BROKEN, YET NEVER SUNDERED

BROKEN, YET NEVER SUNDERED

Orthodox Witness and the Ecumenical Movement

by

Gregory C. Wingenbach

Holy Cross Orthodox Press
Brookline, Massachusetts 02146

Funds for the publication of this book were graciously provided by the

ARCHBISHOP IAKOVOS EDUCATION FUND

and by an Anonymous donor

© Copyright 1987 by Holy Cross Orthodox Press

Published by Holy Cross Orthodox Press
50 Goddard Avenue
Brookline, Massachusetts 02146

Cover design by John N. Vaporis

Library of Congress Cataloging-in-Publication Data

Wingenbach, Gregory Charles, 1938-
Broken, yet never sundered.

Bibliography: p.
Includes index
1. Christian union—Orthodox Eastern Church.
2. Orthodox Eastern Church—
Doctrines. I. Title.
BX324.W56   1987 281.9 87-3048
ISBN 0-917651-28-6 (pbk.)

CONTENTS

Abbreviations of Books Frequently Referred to in the Text

AGL   *The Analytical Greek Lexicon* (Grand Rapids, 1975).

AF-G   *The Apostolic Fathers: A New Translation and Commentary,* ed. Robert M. Grant, Vols. 1-6 (New York, 1964).

AF-S   *The Apostolic Fathers,* ed. Jack N. Sparks (Nashville, 1978).

CJC   *The Early Church and the World,* C. J. Cadoux (Edinburgh, 1925).

ECF/B   *The Early Christian Fathers,* ed. and trans. Henry Bettenson (London, 1969).

FEF/J   *The Faith of the Early Fathers,* trans. William A. Jurgens, Vols. 1-3 (Collegeville, Minn., 1970).

G-EL/NT   *A Greek-English Lexicon of the New Testament and Other Early Christian Literature,* ed. William F. Arndt and F. Wilbur Gingrich (Chicago/Grand Rapids, 1974).

JBC   *The Jerome Biblical Commentary,* ed. Raymond E. Brown, S.S., Joseph A. Fitzmyer, S.J., and Roland E. Murphy, O.Carm. (Englewood Cliffs, N.J., 1968).

LCF/B   *The Later Christian Fathers,* ed. and trans. Henry Bettenson (London, 1970).

Love/N.T.   *The Love Command in the New Testament,* Victor Paul Furnish (Nashville, 1972).

The *Rudder*   The *Rudder (Pedalion): All the Sacred and Divine Canons of the One, Holy, Catholic and Apostolic Church,* English edition, ed. and annot. D. Cummings (Chicago, 1957).

7 Ecum. Councils *The Seven Ecumenical Councils,* from *A Select Library of Nicene and Post-Nicene Fathers of the Christian Church,* Vol. 14 (Grand Rapids, 1971).

Introduction

This study highlights the authentic ecumenical Tradition of the Orthodox Catholic Church as a stream of ministry which is no less than a principal tributary of her source—Jesus Christ's evangelical mission to the world. The purpose of this study is, first of all, to help those engaged in this vital ministry and, secondly, to increase self-understanding and a keener missionary sense among the Orthodox faithful. Nevertheless, a disclaimer is in order: this is not intended as a definitive history or exposition of ecumenism, nor as polemic for or against contemporary trends and movements within it.

The debate within Orthodoxy's worldwide family regarding the ecumenical movement is being waged only partly in reference to the Church's own historic Tradition. In part, controversy has arisen simply because Orthodox involvement has multiplied many times over during the past sixty years. Also, contemporary Orthodox ecumenical activities have been conceived, executed, and sustained throughout largely by a select cadre of hierarchs and theologians and undertaken more often than not in reaction to Protestant initiatives. Since such activities—as well as reactions to others' initiatives—have likewise involved little practical commitment on the part of the faithful (or even of the clergy and hierarchy as a whole), a serious gap exists in the perception of ecumenism and its very roots.

Therefore, many Orthodox have difficulty perceiving Orthodoxy's underlying ecumenical ideology and practice as being in the context of what, for two thousand years, has been her normative guide: the Holy Scriptures, Ecumenical Synods and Fathers, Eucharistic Divine Liturgy, and Sacraments. These authorities, woven together into a whole fabric, constitute the historic Covenant (Tradition) of the Catholic Church. To borrow Father Bruce Vawter's felicitous description of prophecy, the Covenant of Orthodoxy is "the living Word of a living God, a continually living and growing reality"[1] in the life of the world. As Christ Himself is "the Word made flesh that dwelt amongst us"(Jn 1.14), so the Covenant has taken flesh in the experience of God's faithful people. As the existential "Canon within the canon"[2] which is universally authoritative, it is not to be confused with mere archival records of the past or even revered ancient mores. The latter, being only human "traditions of the elders," may guide particular peoples and cultures and may, at least for a while, serve them well; yet, such traditions are not necessarily relevant to or binding on the whole. More so perhaps than in any other communion or religious system held among humankind, this sense of a lasting and catholic Tradition guides Orthodoxy in Church and society alike.

Critiques of ecumenism need to be answered in terms of the Covenant, especially if the activity in question is to be perceived as an integral part of the *consensus fidelium*—the faithful experience and reception, in trust and catholicity, of the Church's teachings of the Way in the life of the People of God. Orthodox clergy and laypersons as a whole, whether for, against, or indifferent to the ecumenical movement, are only vaguely aware of the ecumenical nature *per se* of Orthodoxy and of her Churches' essential fidelity to their evangelical and catholic roots in pressing ahead with contemporary ecumenism. There is the risk, then, that the perception will take hold that contemporary ecumenism is, at best, a serendipitous involvement primarily of interest to an elite. At worst, it would be seen as constituting a radical departure from the Church's mission and being.

In defense, some suggest that Orthodoxy's ecumenical statements and programs invariably appeal to the mandate in the Holy Scriptures and historic creeds for the unity of the holy, catholic, and apostolic Church in Christ. Of and by themselves, however, neither such projections of the Church's stance, nor the few positive publications that do exist in the public realm, are adequate to the task. They are insufficient, being couched in very general terms, and make more frequent reference to recent hierarchical encyclicals and actions than to the precedents and roots within Orthodoxy herself.

By contrast, most popular literature on the ecumenical movement and Orthodoxy's involvement is negative. Based on some traditionalist groups' and influential persons' impressions of what has happened and why, these publications tend to equate the pursuits and advocacies of various non-Orthodox groups with Orthodox ecumenists' own actions and views. Many traditionalists also tend to be very selective and eisegetical in proof-texting of the Scriptures and the ancient conciliar and patristic sources. This approach is illustrated by the following statements, issued by Orthodoxy's rigorously fundamentalist wing in opposition to ecumenism. The first is excerpted from a tract by the "Brotherhood of Saint Mark of Ephesos," and the second derives from encyclicals that voice the alarmed views and concerns of the hierarchs comprising the "Russian Orthodox Church Synod in Exile":

> The most dangerous enemy which the Orthodox Church has ever faced is the ecumenical movement, a product of the twentieth century. The ideas which animate this movement are exceedingly simple, yet they were unheard of for over 1900 years. . . . The ecumenists desire to convert all men to their religion and their humanist cause [rather than to] the Orthodox Way . . . the eternal Kingdom of Jesus Christ, which is not of this world.

> Ecumenism is the heresy of heresies because until now every heresy in the history of the Church tried to take over the place of the true Church, while the ecumenical movement, uniting all the heresies, invites them all together to honor themselves as the one, true Church.[3]

> The Tradition of the Church and the examples of the Holy Fathers teach us that the Church holds no dialogues with those who have separated themselves from Orthodoxy . . . and beforehand rejects any compromise with them. . . .[4]

> You [the ecumenically active Orthodox bishops] are uniting with the heterodox not in truth but in indifference to it . . . [in contrast to] the Holy Fathers of the Church [who] did not build on compromises but on firm adherence to the traditions and every iota of the divine dogmas . . . [in this way] manifesting true love toward the heterodox . . . in their zeal to enlighten them with the light of truth and in caring for their genuine reunion with the Holy Church.[5]

These perceptions of Orthodoxy, the Church Fathers, and ecumenism, as I intend to demonstrate in the course of this study, are not representative of the Church's actual covenantal and evangelical history. The record of the Church's ecumenical tradition clearly shows that, while fiercely protective of her integrity, the Fathers were generally anything but monolithic and unyielding in response to the various heterodox, schismatic, heretical, and non-Christian movements and persons. As we shall see, had the former indeed shown themselves to be so rigid pastorally, the Church would have disowned them as she did the Donatists and other puritan varieties, as being false to the catholic witness of the Holy Scriptures and especially to the Messiah whom they professed as the Word of the universal Father.

Still, enough of a grain of truth is evident in this minority's exposition, particularly in the absence of readily available information to the contrary. Their articulate, impassioned arguments frequently carry the day or plant a plausible seed of doubt among zealous clergy and laity who are apprehensive about the health of the Church and her spiritual life in a pluralistic, humanist-centered society. One pastor and theologian who speaks for this body of concern, Father Michael Azkoul, some years ago suggested:

> If there is anyone who can offer a new art, a new music, a new worship, new letters, new laws and a new piety which more compellingly and beautifully penetrates to the mysteries of God and His divine Oeconomia than that which has traditionally been associated with Orthodoxy, we shall leap to consume them. . . .

> We are not so naive that we fail to recognize that, at the human level, error and superstition and nationalist accommodation have crept into the Orthodox Church; and we have not the slightest doubt that the personal understanding of the Orthodox faithful will be deepened and purified by every new circumstance of the Church. But we shall not betray the blood and agony of the past and present . . . [nor] tear the historical heart and root from the Church and [thereby] set

the People of God adrift upon the capricious currents of heresy, compromise and apostasy. . . .

Syncretism and eclecticism is not catholicism; it is conservatism that has maintained the catholic and sobornost nature of the Church. Our Christ is the Christ of cosmic history, the Christ of the Fathers, the incarnate Logos. We reject both the predestination Christ and the legalist Christ of the juridical Atonement. *Cur Deus homo?* . . . God became man that man might become god, freely, by Uncreated Grace of the divine Trinity in the Church of Truth.[6]

Father Azkoul's sentiments suggest a genuine degree of openness, tempered by an equally genuine caution and even a fear. Insisting on the Church's historical being and evangelical witness, in this respect he and others of like concern probably represent a core of Orthodox consensus. This concern has, by the former's own witness, been heightened by the controversies over various actions and movements underway in recent times among non-Orthodox communions, including the Roman Catholic Church and mainstream Protestant confessional bodies, which are the leading participants in modern ecumenism. Father Azkoul and other critics perceive these trends as being less in the nature of renewal and more in the nature of widespread rejection of the Church's most basic Christian Tradition and enduring values, apparently undertaken in order to accommodate a humanistic society's changing mores and demands. This, in turn, colors their view of the ecumenical movement itself.

According to historical evidence, such deep-seated apprehension was present at the time of the several late medieval attempts to reunite the Eastern and Western Churches. Many scholars[7] feel that these attempts failed for four reasons: first, few of the principal leaders entered into the enterprise either with a sense of pastoral economy or with serious hopes for reconciliation; second, fewer still had sufficient care for or knowledge of the whole of the Church's Tradition, including the patristic example of catholic diversity-in-unity which might have helped to heal the breach;[8]

third, the efforts were frustrated by mutual monologue, fostered by rigorist factions in both camps and by lack of a *consensus fidelium* that could assure the people's trust of the outcome; and fourth, underlying issues behind crucial questions were evaded or treated on a superficial, "pragmatic" level. The primary such question involved the fundamental schism in East/West ecclesial development and theological outlook in the wake of Europe's scholastic movement. Others included the implications, to the Church as a whole, of the emerging papal autocracy and the juridical approach to church life which came into opposition with the ancient Christian patrimony of local autonomy, collegial decision-making, and diversity of expression and practices.

It is not, however, the function of this study to review the sad, though instructive, history of the medieval ecumenical movement. It is a fact that, although interchurch contact has increased immensely and interconfessional dialogues have become both more sustained and wide-ranging in this century, parallels still exist between then and now. These parallels warrant a sense of urgency, especially of the needs to increase mutual ecumenical awareness and education and to deepen the commitment in terms of the Church's historic guidelines and her sense of catholicity.

That the enterprise is uneasy and the trust is shaky we find increasingly evident today. Notice, for example: (1) various recent conferences of ecumenical leaders, the aim of which appears to be more to reassure the participants themselves and, secondarily, to convince a watching world that "all is well, after all";[9] (2) the apprehensive encyclicals addressed by the pioneer ecumenical Churches of Constantinople and Greece to the World Council of Churches (1973 and 1978, respectively);[10] and (3) the confrontation in 1981 between Orthodox member delegations and the World Council's executive committee and secretariat. In the course of the latter, an unprecedented encounter of frankly expressed concern, the entire Orthodox caucus complained of "a perceived imbalance favoring Protestant Churches" over Orthodox in ecumenical representation at key levels and activities, in issues and theological issuances alike, in language employed, and in overall conciliar methodology.[11] This situation is offset only partially by the equally unprecedented ecumenical advances which have been achieved recently on several fronts. For the first time in exactly eleven centuries, official international unity talks have been instituted *on an equal and equitable basis* between the separated sister Churches of Orthodoxy and Roman Catholicism.[12] After decades of persistent dialogue among Orthodox, Protestant, Anglican, and Roman Catholic theologians, unanimous consensus was reached early in 1982 (Faith and Order Commission, World Council of Churches, at Lima, Peru) on ecumenical approaches to the crucial issues of Baptism, the Eucharist, and Ministry in the Church.[13] Also, openings in dialogue and even evidences of mutual concern and theological consensus are now beginning between representative bodies of conservative Evangelical Reformed tradition and the Orthodox and Roman Catholic Churches. As indicated above, however, these partial advances could yet be jeoparidized by the widespread lack of a *consensus fidelium* among the latter and in the Christian world at large.

The Questions at Issue

An informed survey can make a positive contribution to the quality of the current debate, especially among the Orthodox and Roman Catholic Churches, and fill a gap in the extant literature available. With this in mind, this study addresses three central questions:

1. How integral and historic are the roots of ecumenism, and the justification therof, in the Church's authentic Covenant: scriptural, conciliar and patristic, canonical, and sacramental? What are they?

2. Orthodox ecclesiology has traditionally seen the Church[14] as: the living Body of Christ, known and experienced as an historical reality of the Kingdom of God among us, rather than as some invisible spiritual entity or merely as an eschatological ideal, somehow to be realized in a distant future . . . diverse in local Churches and expression, yet always united as One in the Lord's own *mysterion* of the Eucharistic assembly of eternal remembrance and communion . . . a Body "broken, yet never sundered apart,"[15] a Church always catholic in her evangelical witness and always faithful in continuum of the apostolic succession of Jesus Christ's "Way,

Truth, and Life":

> [How can we, then] accept the assertion . . . that, owing to
> a lack of love among brothers, . . . "the Church which was
> established by Christ to be glorious, without spot or wrinkle,
> perfect and holy," was altered?. . . [Are there, instead] several
> Churches, none of which is fully true and holy . . . ?[16]

This question, posed above by the avowedly anti-ecumenical,
rigorist Metropolitan Philaret (Russian Church in Exile), involves
the problem of Orthodoxy's essential being. In other words, it
asks what does it imply—insofar as Orthodoxy's self-identity
as the *Una Sancta Ecclesia*—when she participates as an ecclesiastical partner in modern organic, interconfessional, and quasi-
conciliar ecumenism and when a plurality of her official spokesmen acknowledge an at least *de facto* recognition of other, separated bodies as actual churches and communions (however imperfectly realized) within the historic Judaeo-Christian Tradition?

3. Based on precedents in church life and history, what limits
as well as what flexibility ought normally to govern the various
policies and activities of the Orthodox Churches within the contemporary ecumenical movement and in their mission of evangeliza-
tion? There is, on the one hand, the principle originally expressed
in the very first ecumenical encyclical of modern times, addressed
by the Patriarchate of Constantinople (1902) as she cautioned potential laborers in the vineyard: "We must guard in integrity . . . the
dogmas of the Orthodox Faith [and] safeguard the whole external
life of Orthodoxy."[17]

On the other hand, in the conserving yet open spirit which
Father Azkoul expressed, as well as according to the pastoral mind
of the ancient Fathers, the Church has the necessity not to bind
in things which are nonessential, realizing that a rigorist approach
in all situations may be the occasion, not for spiritual growth and
closer communion in Christ, but for scandal and disheartenment.
As the wise householder in Christ, the Church must "bring out
of her treasure both what is new and old"(Mt.13.52). One Greek
Orthodox theologian suggests that the Church faces challenges today as never before:

Dogmas are signposts that point us on our way and prevent us from slipping into pitfalls of error, [yet] they do not exclude further theologizing. . . . It is a mistake to think . . . that the [Councils'] dogmatic pronouncements constitute a prohibition. . . .

Several teachings in the Orthodox Catholic Church . . . demand being thought through anew—not in order to be reassessed, . . . but rather to be reaffirmed with greater clarity, . . . [for the] Reformation produced . . . theological debates around truths concerning which Orthodoxy had never . . . expressed her consciousness.

The Church . . . preserves the living Tradition which she receives from the past, relives it, and enriches it with the spiritual experience of the present, in organic growth. . . . There is a task awaiting . . . the members of the Orthodox Catholic Church: that of reliving the Tradition and thus better understanding it and better defining it.[18]

Thus will Orthodoxy be able to help bring about "the well-being and stability of the holy churches of God, and the union of all." [19]

NOTES

[1] *JBC* 12.25, 237.

[2] James A. Sanders, *Torah and Canon* (Philadelphia, 1972), p. 120.

[3] Chrysostomos Stratman and Monk Theodoretos of Mount Athos, *The Ecumenists* (Oak Park, Ill., 1981).

[4] Synodal letters, respectively, to Ecumenical Patriarch Athenagoras I of Constantinople, dated Christmas 1965, and to Greek Orthodox Archbishop Iakovos of America, dated Feast of Orthodoxy 1969.

[5] Ibid.

[6] "Are Conservatives Reactionary?" *LOGOS* (December, 1968), pp. 13-14.

[7] See: Deno John Geanakoplos, *Byzantine East and Latin West: Two Worlds of Christendom in Middle Ages and Renaissance* (New York and Evanston, 1966); Steven Runciman, *The Eastern Schism: A Study of the Papacy and the Eastern Churches during the Eleventh and Twelfth Centuries* (London, 1970); Francis Dvornik, *The Photian Schism: History and Legend* (London, 1970); Jaroslav Pelikan, *The Christian Tradition, 2: The Spirit of Eastern Christendom (600-1700)* (Chicago, 1977).

[8] Johan Meijer, C. Ss. R., *A Successful Council of Union: A Theological Analysis of the Photian Synod of 879-880,* Analekta Vlatadon, 23. (Thessalonike, 1975).

[9] As, for example: "The Future of the Ecumenical Movement" International Symposium, Brookline, Mass., January 9-12, 1980, reported in *Orthodox Observer,* January 30, 1980, pp. 1 and 3; International Ecumenical Institute, Worcester, Mass., August, 1980, reported in *Journal of Ecumenical Studies,* 17, 1980, 753-56; "Toward a Truly Ecumenical Council" Conference, North American Academy of Ecumenists, Indianapolis, September 26-28, (1980), reported in *Journal of Ecumenical Studies,* 18, (1981), 208-10.

[10] See below Chapter 7: "Orthodox Ecumenical Witness in the Twentieth Century."

[11] Ref. the report in *St. Vladimir's Theological Quarterly,* 25 (1981) 191-204.

[12] Thomas FitzGerald, "A New Phase in Orthodox-Roman Catholic Relations," *Greek Orthodox Theological Review,* 25 (1980) 119-30; and Norman Russell and Louis Bouyer, "Catholic-Orthodox Dialogue: Patmos and Rhodes," *Sobornost,* 3 (1981) 86-92.

[13]William H. Lazareth, "Ecumenical Document on Baptism, Eucharist, and Ministry—A Way to the Future," *Ecumenical Trends,* 11 (1982) 49-53.

[14]See: Lewis J. Patsavos, "The Canon Law of the Orthodox Catholic Church: Unpublished Notes" (Brookline, Mass.: Holy Cross School of Theology, 1975), esp. pp. 2-7; Georges Florovsky, *Bible, Church, Tradition: An Eastern Orthodox View* (Belmont, Mass., 1972); Alexander Schmemann, *Sacraments and Orthodoxy* (Montreal, 1965); Demetrios J. Constantelos, *Understanding the Greek Orthodox Church* (New York, 1982); Metropolitan Chrysostomos of Myra, "Authority in the Orthodox Church," *Sobornost,* 3 (1981) 197-209.

[15]From the celebrant's Communion Prayers in the Eucharistic Divine Liturgy of the Orthodox Church.

[16]Ibid. above, letter to Archbishop Iakovos.

[17]Constantin G. Patelos (ed.), *The Orthodox Church in the Ecumenical Movement,* (Geneva, 1978), pp. 27-33.

[18]Eusebius Stephanou, *The Orthodox Church and the Ecumenical Movement* (Brookline, Mass., n.d.) pp.10-11, 12-13.

[19]From the Great Litany of Peace which begins the Vespers service, the Eucharistic Divine Liturgy, and other major Sacraments and services of the Orthodox Church.

CHAPTER ONE:
Torah and the Lord's Covenant

One form of biblical literature is the prophetic sermon (*torah*), a collection of sayings cast within a common context and relevant to a single theme. It takes the form of a catena, or chain, in order to communicate an essential understanding of the common identity and relationship of different segments more succinctly and poetically. The following *torah* is such an anthology, culled from the Scriptures of the Old Testament to illustrate the growing reality of the evangelical and ecumenical theme within the prophetic consciousness of ancient Israel and the *oikoumene:*[1]

> The earth is the Lord's, and all within,
> the world and those who dwell therein.
> In the hands of the Lord are
> the souls of the living, all of humankind.
> Sing to the Lord, all peoples of the earth,
> bless the Lord and exalt Him forever!

> He Who created the skies and made the earth
> and all that grows in it,
> He Who made man in God's own image and likeness,
> male and female He made them and blessed them,
> He Who gave breath to the peoples of the earth,
> the breath of life to all who walk upon it,
> The same Lord Who is God speaks:

> I now make My Covenant with you
> and with your descendants after you,
> with all that live on earth,
> to endless generations.
> I will fulfill My Covenant: for your part
> you must keep My Covenant, you and
> your descendants, generation by generation.

Before I formed you in the womb,
  I knew you for My own;
Before you were born,
    I consecrated and appointed you
    to be a Prophet to all the nations,
    a Covenant to all peoples,
    a beacon for the nations:
    to bring good news to the poor and lowly,
    and to heal the broken-hearted,
    to proclaim release to the captives,
    and to give sight to the blind,
    to proclaim liberty to those
    who lay in dungeons of darkness.
Bring everyone who is called by My Name,
  all whom I have created and formed,
  all whom I have made for My glory,
  that My salvation may reach
  to the farthest bounds of the earth.

You, My servants, are My witnesses
  whom I have chosen
  to know Me,
  to put your faith in Me,
  and to understand that
I am He, I am God, the Lord,
  your Holy One,
  your Creator, Israel, your King.

Thereafter the day shall come
  when I shall pour out My Spirit
  upon all of humankind.
Then I Myself will come
  to gather all nations and races;
Then will I lead the blind ones on their way,
  and guide them by paths which they know not;
I will turn darkness into light before them
  and straighten their twisting roads.

All this will I do, leaving nothing undone.

Some I will send to the nations
    which have never yet heard of Me
    nor yet seen My glory;
These shall announce that glory
    among the nations:
Gather together, come, draw near,
    all you nations.
Come forward and put forth your case
    let us consult,
    let us reason together.

Look to Me and be saved, says the Lord,
    you peoples from all corners of the earth!
For I have given a promise of victory,
    one that will not be broken: that
    to Me every knee shall bend, and
    by Me every tongue shall pledge true word.

All the nations shall come
    in procession to the House of the Lord;
Many peoples shall come:
    One shall say, "I am the Lord's own,"
    and another shall write the Lord's Name
    on his hand
    and to his own add the Name of Israel.

These will I bring to My holy hill,
    and give joy to them in My House of prayer.
Their offerings and sacrifices
    shall be acceptable on My altar,
    for My House shall be called
    a House of prayer for all the nations.

This is the very word of the Lord God,

Who brings home the dispersed of Israel:
I will yet bring home
   all that remain to be brought in;
I will give all peoples once again pure lips,
   that they may invoke the Lord by Name
   and serve Him with one consent.

"There is nothing new under the sun," the ancient writer of Ecclesiastes (1.9) tells us. So, too, as the *torah* above witnesses, the ecumenical impulse, which aims to assemble as one "all humankind . . . from all corners of the earth," is nothing new. Ecumenism is an evangelical movement to restore wholeness to a broken world, and as such it is as ancient as God's own relationship with humankind. Its font and focal point is the promise which He made of His kingdom to those whom He has created and who, just as importantly, "hold true His Covenant." With the Prophets, ecumenical Christians protest in a divided world that "we all have one Father, one God Who created us" and that we are bound, in His Name, to "reason together" and to work and pray for unity in Him.

All of this would seem to indicate, then, that the ecumenical movement cannot be viewed as some insidious "modernist heresy." Nor, even on a totally positive note, can it be equated with diverse contemporary manifestations, i.e., the World and National Councils of Churches and their various predecessors or offspring, the Vatican II Church Council of modern Roman Catholicism, etc. What these activities do show is that during the past half-century or so ecumenism has visibly been experiencing its most vigorous season, through the vehicle of

a movement, expressed in a wide variety of activities and programs and institutions, aiming at the unity and reconciliation . . . which our Lord wills for all persons, . . . ebbing

and flowing in a variety of directions and expressing itself
in diverse ways.[2]

Conversely, ecumenism as a concrete ideal and force is by no
means limited to the particular scope, philosophy, or history of
these modern ecumenical phenomena, because it is basic and its
roots are found deep in the ground of man's being, God and His
creation.

Yahweh's Bond of "Covenant Love"

The ancient Hebrews were all too familiar with division, separation, dissension, syncretism, assimilation, and other manifestations of disunity and "breaking faith" among those whom the Lord
had created, especially the Chosen People of Israel. But that was
the negative side. The positive relationship of which disunity and
heresy were violation and sin is covenant, expressed primarily
in two complementary terms: *berit* (συνθήκη) and *hesed we'emet*
(κοινωνία).[3]

Berit is the principle and the fact of Israel's unity as a people,
commonly bound together in trust and obligation with Yahweh
and one another. In certain periods of their history, fierce patriotism
and exclusivism were necessary to motivate a people beleaguered
in the midst of a hostile sea of polytheism which would dim their
consciousness of the diversity of God's creation. But, at least in
Joshua, Judges, and the monarchy, Israel consciously included
groups of different origins that had come by diverse paths into
the way of the Lord Yahweh. The scions of Abraham, Isaac, and
Jacob who shared the Egyptian captivity, the Exodus, and the set-
tlement of the Promised Land were joined in covenant with the
Habiru, Jebusites, and others who had not done so. As the
Prophets witness, blood was not the sole criterion for covenant:

> Let not the foreigner,
> who has given to the Lord his allegiance, say,

"The Lord will keep me separate
forever from His People."
Nor must the eunuch say,
"I am naught but a barren tree."

For these are the words of the Lord:
"Who chooses to do My will
    and holds true My Covenant, . . .
    shall receive from Me . . .
A name in My own House and within My walls . . .
    joy in My House of prayer . . .
for My House shall be called
    a House of prayer for all the nations. . . ."

(Is 56.3-7)

By accepting the Covenant of Yahweh with Israel, others were joined in unity with the whole, and "the traditions of Yahweh's saving acts . . . the obligations of the Covenant" became those of the entire group.[4] The unity was religious, not ethnic. The worship of Yahweh alone as the one Lord and God of all, the traditions of the Mosaic Law, and the Holiness Code are the unifying norm, as seen in the sealing of the Shechem covenant (Jos 24).

The marriage of these diverse peoples and the maintenance of a stable bond within the nation of Israel required a cement that went beyond mere confederation of contractual obligation in the formal sense. This was found in *hesed we'emet*: a steadfast "covenant love"[5] of spiritual kinship that is realized among a people of closely-shared tradition, common will toward group survival, identity, and growth in the face of ever-hostile surroundings, and a kindness and morality in human relations that surpasses the minimum, required duties. In this spirit of "covenant love" is the testimony of the seer of Ecclesiasticus (25.1): ". . . beautiful in the eyes of the Lord and of men are concord among brethren, friendship among neighbors, and a man and a wife who are inseparable." Woe, therefore, is disunity: "detestable to the Lord is the scoundrel, a mischievous man who prowls about stirring up division all the time . . . [and] making quarrels between brethren" (Prov 6.12-19).

In the interest of survival and cohesiveness, an exclusivism naturally takes hold to a significant degree. Assimilation and intermarriage with elements of the surrounding pagan environment, as well as syncretism of creed and cult and mores, are forbidden. Commerce beyond what is absolutely necessary with the Gentiles, those "unclean" nations and peoples who worship foreign gods and practice ways alien to Yahweh and the Law of Moses, is to be shunned. Later, this exclusivism takes an even narrower, sectarian form for some, as Jews of the Qumran community evolved an understanding of Yahweh's covenant as a puritan congregation of persons and small groups who live together strictly according to a particularist communal code of rigorist traditions. This *yahad,* as it was called, constituted a more or less total rejection of the world around them, including Jews who had, in their eyes, strayed from the Way. This development was, understandably, the fruit of centuries of alienation and oppression.

Yahweh, Lord of the Oikoumene

Nevertheless, "Judaism contained within itself the germs of universalism," C. J. Cadoux observes. "The very idea of the one God of all the earth, . . . involved the ultimate inclusion of the Gentiles in the divine blessings." [6] Yahweh is not a tribal god: He is "the Lord our sovereign . . . glorious in all the earth, [Who] looks out from heaven and sees all the inhabitants of earth" (Ps 8.1, 33.13-14).

The promise in Genesis, through the great covenant with Noah and even the less expansive one with Abraham, is for a potentially worldwide covenant of God with all the peoples descended from the great patriarchs. This is a realization of greater wholeness to be sought after, which is never totally forgotten or lost sight of. The ancient memory of the unity of all those whom God has "created and formed" lives on.

The Prophets, above all, chide and remind, challenge and inspire the Chosen People as an antidote to the prideful temptation of tribal exclusivism and sectarian spirit. The Prophets' call also involves the use of both "carrot and stick," potential blessing and curse dangling before remnant Israel's eyes. By the time of the prophetic era, they are a people sorely disunited: the Covenant of the Chosen is strained to and past the breaking point. On the one hand, Israel is warned that Yahweh can elect yet another, more faithful people in their place. On the other hand, God's revelation of His Kingdom and the ensuing salvation of the world can and will be achieved only through the agency of Israel: that is the promise of Yahweh to those whom He has chosen. The means by which this "revelation to the Gentiles" is to take place through Israel remains unknown; subsequently, in the later prophetic and intertestamental eras, it becomes a matter of intense speculation and, inevitably, the occasion for the rise of messianic figures. Deutero-Isaiah warns the people not to dwell on the "hows and wherefores." The messianic mission partakes of the very nature of God's Being and His election of ways and means and persons to bring about His holy purpose. It is sufficient for Israel to turn humbly to "seek the Lord . . . bend your ears, come and listen," for God's ways are far beyond mortal man's comprehension:[7]

> For My thoughts are not your thoughts,
>   nor are My ways your ways.
> This is the very word of the Lord:
>   as the heavens are higher than the earth,
> so My ways are higher than your ways
>   and My thoughts than your thoughts.
>
>   (Is 55.8-9)

During the Exile and afterwards, the realization returns gradually to Israel that Yahweh's claim to universal lordship, indeed His very being as God, is cast in jeopardy and cannot be fulfilled unless His glory is recognized by "all the peoples . . . from all corners of the earth." Expanding on the covenant with Noah and then with Joshua at Shechem, the promise is made to those nations who do accept Yahweh. If His Covenant will be adopted, they, too, will share in the fullness of the gifts and mission bestowed upon Israel from of old. The ancient patrimony is reaffirmed: Abraham, their forefather, had originally been summoned to leave behind his ancestral homeland, settled ways, and even his own native people in order to establish the Chosen People "as an alien . . . in Canaan, . . . in the country of the Philistines [and] the Hittites" (Gen 12-23).

As Abraham's heir, Israel is likewise recalled from its settled ways. No more can Israel be satisfied with merely "holding true the Covenant" and carrying out the prescriptions of the Mosaic Law, but it must embrace anew the missionary vocation of "mediating the knowledge of Yahweh to the nations."[8] To a degree, this does begin to take place. Largely through the fortuitous medium of the classical *oikoumene* (i.e., Hellenistic and Roman culture, commerce, and empires), the presence of tiny despised Israel and the influence of Yahweh's moral code begin increasingly to have impact.

Monotheism is a concept that slowly draws support, particularly among Gentile philosophers and others in the educated and ruling classes who have become disenchanted by crude tales of anthropomorphic and venal gods, magicians, an endless variety of mystery religions, and the swift decline of morality that is occurring. Also, a discreet effort at proselytizing has begun to take hold, mostly in the Hellenistic communities of Jews in the diaspora, settled in Gentile lands. The opportunity, it seems, is ripe, and the ground fertile:[9]

> Arise, Jerusalem, rise clothed in light,
>   your light has come. . . .
> The Lord shall shine upon you,
>   and over you
>   shall His glory appear, . . .
> The nations shall march towards your light
>   and their kings to your sunrise. . . .
>
> The Lord shall proclaim with His own lips
>   a new name, . . .
>   the new heaven and the new earth. . . .
>   (Is 60.1-3, 62.2, 66.22)

Yahweh's New Wine: Not for Old Wineskins

Despite this full promise of the greater future awaiting a messianic Israel, four key factors continued to mute and frustrate Israel's ecumenical witness of her monotheistic faith and moral codes:

1. The particular cultic requirements of the Mosaic Law, uniformly applied to all Gentiles who might wish to share fully—not merely stand as observers in the "outer Temple"—in Israel's Covenant with Yahweh. These requirements were further complicated by accretion over the centuries of the "traditions of the elders," interpreted as binding upon all.

2. The partly canonical, partly ethnic prescriptions for the people's basic isolation from the Gentile world, which inhibited significant contact with the uncircumcised, the unbelievers, and even heterodox kinfolk like the Samaritans.

3. The related attitude which regarded the philosophy and lore of the Gentile world, *in toto,* as "unclean" or, at best, irrelevant, containing no potential truth or having any possible value to the fruitful, covenanted son of Abraham, Isaac, and Jacob.

4. Finally, the favor which the polytheistic cults and religions enjoyed with the state authorities, along with the fact that many allowed a place in their cultic rites for worship of the Emperor or King as a demi-god. This was something by which no true son or daughter of Israel could abide.

In any case, though in ways unknown, Israel's vocation was to be the vessel for the revelation of Yahweh, the one and universal God, to the nations. In terms of God's faithful Covenant, after all, He can only be revealed through those who know Him, and no one could possibly know Yahweh so intimately as Israel. But the revelation of His Being would and does require contact with those who are to learn to know Him. Dialogue is required that may allow the different parties, "I to Thou," truly to encounter one another[10] and to "reason together" in fidelity to Yahweh. This contact can only be achieved by means of "a developing process, [for] no person can be known through a single encounter," least of all Yahweh, who "reveals Himself, not propositions [or] purely intellectual knowledge."[11]

The old wineskins of Israel and Judaism, as then constituted and inhibited as they were, were unable to function as proper vessels for the new wine of Yahweh, for He must reach out in the close encounter of sustained mission, act directly, and be proclaimed among the nations.

NOTES

[1]Torah sources, in order: Ps 24.1, Job 12.10; Ps 96.1/ Dan 3: "Song of the Three"; Is 42.5; Gen 1.26-28/5.1-2, 9.8 & 17, 17.7 & 9; Jer 1.4-5; Is 42.6-7/61.1, 42.7, 49.6. 43.10,13,15; Is 44.5, 56.7-8; Zeph. 3.9. Like similar Biblical anthologies of sayings, this is not intended to be all-inclusive, in precise chronological order, or constitute a proof text.

[2]Robert G. Stephanopoulos (ed.), *Guidelines for Orthodox Christians in Ecumenical Relations,* (New York, 1973), pp.1-2.

[3]*JBC* 77:95-98, 79:115, 752-53, 820.

[4]Ibid. Also, *Torah and Canon, ibid.* above, pp. 17-19.

[5]*JBC,* ibid.

[6]*The Early Church and the World* (Edinburgh, 1925), p. 7.

[7]*JBC* 22:46-49, 379-80.

[8]*JBC* 77:117, 756.

[9]*JBC* 22:60, 68, 70, 383, 385-86 passim.

[10]In the sense observed by Jewish theologian Martin Buber in his *I and Thou,* trans. Walter Kaufmann (New York, 1970), pp. 59, 149-51, 155-57.

[11]*JBC* 77:103-06, 754.

CHAPTER TWO

The Covenant and the Messiah

Perhaps the most distinctive hallmark of Judaism and Christianity alike, seen as two faces of the one Covenant of Yahweh, is that at root they are incarnational and historical. Neither is a philosophy of scholars,[1] gnostic magic and Docetism,[2] or the folk morality of naturalistic humanism.[3] In Judaism and Christianity God exercises a covenantal, saving relationship in which He acts together with, in the midst of, and using the very elements of humankind, nature, and history.

There is no mighty revelation, followed by a pouting desertion, no rude break with history, nor any irrational eruption into the affairs of humankind. There is not stagnation, but growth, as God in His Covenant takes hold of that which already exists in the world and perseveres. A saving remnant, inspired by God, mediates for Him and for the society in which they live and work.

For Saint Athanasios of Alexandria and other Church Fathers, as a matter of fact, the only satisfactory way for God to be in character and truly faithful to the humanity which He had "created and formed"—especially to His Covenant with Israel—was by means of that very act of Incarnation which so scandalized the Jews of Jesus's day. It continues to be the crucial "stumbling-block" between Christians and Jews. The Messiah was and is the One sent by God: according to the Fathers, His coming among men is the eminently logical act of continuity with the ancient covenants which Yahweh made with Noah, Abraham, Moses, and Jacob. By God's deliberate design and in faithful covenant, Abraham left his homeland and raised up a godly nation in the midst of unbelieving nations, Joseph took up his stewardship and prospered in Egypt, and Moses fulfilled his calling as the liberator of the People of God in Egypt and the Exodus. All three fulfilled the will of God by "mediating [His] knowledge to the nations."

The story of Christianity, therefore, is the culminating act of fulfillment of the Old Testament and Yahweh's covenants:

O Christ our God, Thou Who art the fulfillment of the Law
and the Prophets and did accomplish all of the Father's plan
for our salvation, so now fill our hearts with joy and gladness:
now and forever, and unto the ages of ages. Amen.[4]

A favorite theme of the early Fathers is that "God became flesh
and dwelt amongst us"(Jn 1.14), coming as man in a crucial period
of history "in order to renew the state of being 'in the image.' "[5]
The time was ripe in that pivotal world of Israel, as the Jews came
into increasing confrontation and contact with Rome, Hellenism,
and the barbarians, for the Messiah to fulfill the promise of the
ancient Prophets. "In the end of the ages [the Son of God] came
down from the Father's bosom," notes Saint Athanasios, "and from
the undefiled young Jewish maiden Mary took upon Himself our
humanity."[6]

Israel was accustomed to hearing the prophetic word and God's
statutes in the context of human history, by means of real flesh-
and-blood persons who shared Israel's Covenant with Yahweh. This
was in contrast to the lightning-bolt, unilateral divine fiat or the
agency of spirits, demiurges, gods, and the arts of divination so
familiar to the votaries of pagan and mystery religions.[7] The Incarnation and ministry of Jesus the Messiah, the Fathers testify,
met the Covenant People's normative expectation, for it took place
within the natural order, yet was not limited to it or by it:

> Using the body as an instrument, He became man for our
> sakes [in order] that we may no longer return to earth as
> earth, but, now joined with the Word come from heaven, we
> may be carried up with Him into heaven.[8]

Jesus—Archetype of the Covenant's Mission

The Scriptures reveal Jesus to be the Christ Who is the Son
of the universal God and of the Hebrew Prophet-King David, and
thus does He unite within Himself the whole and the particular,
the Divine with the human. He does not disdain our condition,
no matter how fallen, crippled, sinful, compromised, or even far
from Yahweh's Covenant of Faith we may be.[9] In His ministry
among all types and conditions of people—including those judged
by the Law to be "unclean" and forbidden of contact—Jesus can

be seen as the true Archetype of the Church's ecumenical and evangelical mission in this world. Not once did He diminish or dilute God's Word. Yet, He always met human persons and their needs just as they were and wherever they might be:

> And, together with the Twelve, Jesus went about all the cities and villages, preaching and bringing the good news of the Kingdom of God, and healing every disease and infirmity. . . .
>
> When He saw the crowds, He had compassion for them because they were harassed and helpless, as sheep without a shepherd, and He began to teach them many things.
>   (Mt 9.35-37, Mk 6.6,34, Lk 8.l)

Jesus always sought to join people in faith to God's Covenant, so that they might participate in Yahweh's ancient promise of healing, mercy, and wholeness and, in turn, move others to seek His Kingdom. He was always "unwilling to send them away hungry," whether their hunger be physical or spiritual, or both, "lest they faint on the way, for some of them had come a long way" (Mt 15.32, Mk 8.1-3). Indeed, many Jews and Gentiles alike had "come a long way" in their pilgrimage to the Kingdom of God.

Symbolic of this overriding concern were Jesus's dialogues with two very different persons, two types of humankind: Nikodemos, the righteous "man of the Pharisees, a ruler of the Jews" and the Samaritan woman with the checkered past, whom He met at Jacob's well. With them He taps themes that are universal, yet of particular and personal concern to each of these persons whom He encountered in His ministry. As Jesus ministers to the unique need of each, He comments upon the universal spiritual hunger of humankind, quietly reveals His mission as the Messiah of all, and teaches them that no longer may a person be judged solely in terms of law or ritualistic precedent:

> You must be born anew. . . born of the Spirit. . . . For God so loved the world that He gave His only Son, that whoever believes in Him should not perish but have everlasting life. For God sent the Son into the world, not to condemn the world, but that the world might through Him be saved. . . . He who does what is true comes to the light, that it may

be clearly seen that his works have been done in God.

(Jn 3.7-8,17,21)

The nations, as prophesied, will come to Yahweh through the agency of Israel. Jesus tells the Samaritan woman, significantly at the well of one of the universal Fathers of the old Covenant, that a new day has risen for the People of God, for:

> . . . the hour is coming when neither on this mountain nor in Jerusalem will you worship the Father. You worship what you do not know; we worship what we know, for salvation is from the Jews.

> But the hour is coming, and now is at hand, when the true worshipers will worship the Father in spirit and truth, because it is such whom the Father seeks to worship Him. God is spirit, and those who worship Him must worship in spirit and truth. . . . I Who speak to you am [the Messiah].

(Jn 4.21-26)

The Law and the Prophets may not be annulled or simply set aside, as though they were *passè* and of no consequence; the Covenant which they represent is to be fulfilled, i.e., "finished and perfected" by Jesus's own messianic work.[10] Bringing the Covenant to that fulfillment, He has extended "the right to become children of God [to] as many as received Him, . . . [to] those born, not by blood or the will of the flesh and man, but of God" (Jn 1.12-13). Again, this is no radical departure, for such become the *bona fide* children of God through the knowledge of "what the Lord requires: only, to do justice, to love kindness, to walk humbly with your God"(Mic 6.8).

Disciplining the Faithful in "Covenant Love"

That this teaching is not merely a philosophical ideal Jesus makes clear in handling His own relationships, and He so advises the gathered community, in public:

> "Who is My mother? Who are My brothers?" He answered the one who had sought Him out.
> And stretching out His hand toward His disciples, He said,

> "Behold, there are My mother and My brothers! For
> whoever shall do the will of My Father Who is in heaven,
> that one is My brother and sister and mother."
>
> (Mt 12.48-50)

Obviously, then, the sectarian approach of the Essenes is not what
Jesus had in mind. Drawing the line of concern and encounter so
narrowly that it may encompass only those of one's own *yahad*
is, in His interpretation, not a true fulfillment of Yahweh's
Covenant:[11]

> But I say to you, love your enemies and pray for those who
> persecute you, in order that you may be children of your
> Father Who is in heaven. . . .
> For if you love only those who love you, what reward may
> you justly claim?. . . If you greet only your brethren, what
> more do you do than others? Do not even the Gentiles do
> as much?
> Therefore you are to be perfect, as your heavenly Father
> is perfect.
>
> (Mt 5.44-48)

In the ancient world, to "greet" or "salute" (χαίρειν) someone
was to affirm that person's or community's existence in an "I to
Thou" relationship. The other was thereby acknowledged as "subject," rather than as more impersonal "object," and an elemen-
tal bond was affirmed as actually existing between the one greeting
and the one greeted. Both intertestamental writings and the
Evangelist John (in his account of Jesus's last discourse) extend
this relationship to its ultimate potential: fulfillment of the divine
and human love in one, which, even in man's *hamartia* ("missing
of the mark") in carrying out the Covenant, is somehow shared:[12]

> But Thou, our God, art kind and true and patient, a mer-
> ciful ruler of all that is. For even if we sin, we are still Thine;
> we acknowledge Thy power.
>
> (Wis 15.1-2)

> As Thou sent Me into the world, so I sent them into the
> world. . . . Yet it is not for these alone that I pray, but also

for those who believe in me through their word, that they
all may be one, just as Thou, Father, art in Me and I in Thee,
that they, too, may be [one] in Us. Thus the world may believe
that Thou sent Me.

I have even extended to them the glory which Thou has
given Me, that they may be one, just as We are One, I in
them and Thou in Me; that they may be brought to completion as one.

Thus may the world come to know that Thou did send Me
and that Thou loved them, even as Thou has loved Me.

(Jn 17.18-26)

This is Jesus's challenge, by His Father's commission to Him
and by His own "consecration in truth" of His disciples. In fulfilling
Yahweh's mission, Jesus has no intention of "gathering the scattered" by means of His own earthly ministry of such short dura-
tion and scope. He has, rather, inaugurated the Kingdom in this
world; He has not brought it yet to completion, whether in Israel
or among the nations. He has set the example and begun the process only. Now, though in a far grander vision and scope, He returns
to the archetype of the ancient Covenant, whereby a redeemed
remnant is commissioned prophetically as disciples to minister and
bring the good news to the people "who dwell in darkness" (Is
9.1-2, Lk 1.79). Yahweh's light is a gift freely to be extended to
all of humankind, that, greeted in encounter, they all may become
one in His "Way, Truth, and Life," which Jesus identifies with
Himself (Jn 14.6).

Jesus refers to the disciples as His "friends" who do naturally
what He has gathered and called them to: "No longer do I call
you servants[13] for the servant does not know what his master is
doing. I have called you friends, for all things that I have heard
from My Father I have made known to you . . ." (Jn 15.14-16ff).
Friends, moreover, are chosen freely, not assigned or bought as
are servants and slaves whom one cannot reasonably expect to share
in their master's confidence. A true friend is an intimate.

As intimates of the Lord, Jesus's disciples are to be free not
merely from subservience, but likewise from the ignorance of
Yahweh's will and from the uncertainty and despair of those "who

walk in darkness." They are to share directly in their Master's own commission, as ones anointed "to go forth in peace, in the Name of the Lord."[14] In contrast to the withered fig tree which Jesus scorned,[15] furthermore, they are to be fruitful: to make disciples of all humankind and, in "mediating the knowledge of Yahweh to all the nations," transform each and every one "who worships in spirit and truth" into friends and witnesses, no longer servants or slaves.[16]

In modeling the unity of His disciples and "those who believe . . . through their word" in the unity of the divine Father and Son, Jesus is hardly describing some mystical sect, ethical fellowship, or loose confederation of like-minded individuals and groups. His model of unity, by contrast, is that of the very God: organic and to be expressed in a dynamic community which is self-evidently one and visible enough "to challenge the world to believe in Jesus":[17]

> I am the good Shepherd, and I know My own. My own know Me, even as the Father knows Me and I know the Father, and I lay down My life for My sheep.

> And I have other sheep, who are not of this fold. I must bring them in also, and they shall hear my voice, and they shall become one flock with one Shepherd.
>
> (Jn 10.14-16)

There are two key points to be observed in eliciting the meaning here. Again, in the ancient world, "to know" did not mean mere acquaintance or even a sophisticated level of intellectual perception. Analogous to χαίρειν, the idea presupposed an intimate communion of persons which, in heart and mind alike, closely shared in an organic fellowship. Secondly, the coupling of καθὼς and ἵνα ("just as" and "in order/so that") carries both a comparative and causative force: "the heavenly unity is both the model and source of the unity of believers,"[18] that is to say, "the model and principle of the unity of the disciples, since the 'Name' that Christ has revealed is nothing less than the divine life itself [and] to share in this glory."[19] The force of these particular usages identifies both the nature of the divine unity and how Jesus intends for that unity to be manifested among and by humanity, through the Church.

Disunity: "Unless You Abide in Me . . ."

A further indication of the binding, organic unity which Jesus witnesses to is the fact that He denounces and warns against disunity frequently. As in the incident with the withered fig tree, He links disunity to the barrenness of an unproductive organism that is to be despised. Unity, on the other hand, is characterized by worth and His own fruitfulness:

> I am the true Vine, and My Father is the Gardener. Every branch in Me that does not bear fruit, He takes away. Every branch that does bear fruit, He prunes, in order that it may bear still more fruit.
>
> You are already pruned, because of the word that I have spoken to you. Abide in Me, and I in you.
>
> As the branch cannot bear fruit by itself, unless it abides and remains one with the vine, neither can you unless you abide, remaining one with Me.
>
> I am the Vine, and you are the branches. He who abides in Me, and I in Him, bears much fruit, for apart from Me you can do nothing. If anyone does not abide in Me, that one is thrown away just as is a [fruitless] vine branch, drying up and shriveling away. Such are gathered up, cast into the fire, and burned.
>
> If you do abide in Me, and My words abide in you, [know that] you may ask whatever you wish, and it shall be done for you. By this is My Father glorified, in that you bear much fruit and thus prove to be My disciples.
>
> (Jn 15.1-8)

There is diversity in this imagery: the roots, the trunk, the branches, the twigs, the leaves, and each part that goes to make up the whole vine "abides" in its natural integrity and, either well or badly, performs its particular being and function. Yet, of necessity a unity "abides" in all: the Vine is manifestly one, and that whole is Jesus Christ. The disciples will be able to act faithfully and consequently will bear fruit in discipleship. They will be empowered to do so by means of the life-giving *anamnesis* (remembrance) of Christ and His unifying "love which courses through the whole plant":[20]

> And when the Advocate comes [the One Who strengthens and completes with God's Spirit] whom I shall send to you from the Father, [know that] this One is truly the Spirit of truth who proceeds from the Father, being the One Who will give true witness to Me.
>
> (Jn 15.26-27)

The abiding Presence of the life-giving Spirit, God's own Advocate of truth and therefore of unity, will enable the disciples to bear fruit in the often unreceptive, rocky soil of the world. The disciples of Christ constitute the *Ekklesia* (Church), the assembly of the People of God who are gathered together in this world and yet are "not truly of this world." But they are only faithful to their Lord when they are fulfilling their destiny of being sent, just as the Son has been sent by the Father, to gather and bear fruit.[21] Furthermore, this Body can only do so as one:

> Every kingdom divided against itself cannot stand. If a house is divided against itself, that house will not be able to stand.
>
> (Mt 12.25-26,Mk 3.24-25)

Outside of the unity perceived in the Triune type,[22] the Church is obviously crippled, fails to reflect the image of God to which she has been called and in which she was created, and is incapable of truly performing her evangelical mission to the *oikoumene*.

In Saint Matthew's Gospel account (5.13), Jesus asks: "If the salt has lost its savor, with what shall it be made tasteful again?" It is in Saint Mark's account of the same saying (9.50) that He provides His own solution: the Church may only regain her savor as "the salt which gives taste to the earth [if] you have salt in yourselves, and be at peace with one another."

To profess faith truly in "the Son of Man . . . the Messiah, Son of the living God . . . revealed to you by my heavenly Father," Jesus tells Peter, "is the rock [on which] I will build my Church" (Mt 16.13,16-18). For that reason, one's profession of faith cannot ever be a hedging, uncertain, or evasive act; otherwise, the world will not know the Lord and His one Covenant "in spirit and truth." Some of Jesus's followers preferred to hedge and evade, and He turned to other witnesses:

> And Jesus asked His disciples, "Who do men say that the Son of Man is?" They answered, "Some say John the Baptist, others Elijah, others Jeremiah, or one of the Prophets."
> (Mt 16.13-14, Mk 8.27-28, Lk 9.18-19)

Such an indefinite reply did not qualify as anything men could live by, and Jesus showed clearly that "creedless faith" of that sort did not satisfy Him. He persisted, "And what about you: who do you say I am?" This provoked Peter's epochal witness to Jesus as the Messiah. The key to unity is, therefore, revealed to be the realization and undaunted profession by Peter and his colleagues that the prophecies and images of the Messiah come to fulfillment only in Jesus, as the very Son of the God of Abraham, Isaac, and Jacob. By Jesus's own testimony, His Church is actually founded upon the Faith of the Apostles, confessing together as one.

Judge Not, Walk Humbly

But faith and unity go beyond mere creedal profession. It is the doing and fulfilling of the Word which truly builds upon that rock:

> He who hears [My words] and does not do them is like a man who built a house on the ground, without foundation. The stream broke against it, it fell at once, and the ruin of

that house was great.

(Mt 7.26-27, Lk 6.49)

We build even our prayer and worship of Yahweh "on sand, without foundation" if we do not act humbly, if our very being is torn by inner dissension, or if we are troubled by quarrels with our brothers and sisters:

> If you are offering your gift at the Altar, and there you remember that your brother has something against you, leave your gift there before the Altar. Then go and first be reconciled to your brother, and come to offer your gift.
>
> (Mt 5.23-24)

So far as Jesus is concerned, even the Sabbath is not as vital as is this practice of faith in humbleness of heart and reconciliation. "The Sabbath was made for man, not man for the Sabbath," He teaches (Mk 2.27). The whole point of the Sabbath—indeed of all worship—is to do good and to give right praise (*orthodoxia*), in order that people, "seeing your works of good faith, may glorify your Father in heaven" (Mt 5.16).

In fulfillment of the prophetic spirit of the Old Testament, Jesus especially warns us about our natural human propensity to sit in judgment over other people and their actions. Judgment, He says, is a two-edged sword that, in the fallible hands of humankind, can turn against the one too ready to wield it:

> Judge not, and you will not be judged. Do not condemn others, and you will not be condemned. Forgive, and you will be forgiven. Give, and it shall be given unto you [in] good measure, . . . running over into your lap.
>
> (Lk 6.37-38)

> So, whatever you wish that people do to you, do thus to them. This is the Law and the Prophets.
>
> (Mt 7.12)

God alone has the right to judge, for He is resolved to know the truth, "dealing justly [as] the Judge over all the earth" (Gen 18.21,25). The emphasis in the Scriptures is less on God as the supreme, rightful Avenger, for "Yahweh desires not that the wicked man die but that he be converted from his evil ways and live" (Ezek 18.23) in spirit and truth. He has concluded a Covenant with His people, and "by the Covenant God has bound Himself to obtain justice and the good life" for His Chosen People.[23] This is a face of the Old Testament's own teaching and Israel's experience with Yahweh which, Jesus knew, had by this time become neglected. The emphasis by now was more upon the Law's strictures, the "traditions of the elders," and, to a certain extent, the more foreboding side of the later Prophets' apocalyptic visions.

In His integral sense of the Covenant, Jesus neither modified His Evangel nor failed to reproach those who dealt loosely with the Faith. Even so, He, too, is reluctant to be cast in the role of judge. His primary emphasis throughout the Gospels is as Teacher and Saviour. "Who made Me judge over you?" Jesus gently reproaches one man who has sought Him out in a dispute with another (Lk 12.14). If that is His attitude toward His own role, how much more so with His disciples and all others who would come later to claim His Name and take up His "gentle yoke"? He rebukes His disciples several times on account of their pride and the zeal with which they make quick judgments or take on themselves more than is their rightful due. Jesus shows that His concern is pastoral, as He tries to keep the disciples from heading for a fall in the course of their newly-appointed ministry:

> And He sent messengers ahead of Him, who went and entered a village of the Samaritans, to make ready for Him. But the people there would not receive Him, because His face was set toward Jerusalem. And when the disciples, James and John, saw this, they said, "Lord, do you want us to bid fire come down from the heavens and consume these people?" But He turned and rebuked them, and they proceeded toward another village.
>
> (Lk 9.52-56)

The seventy returned with joy, saying, "Lord, even the

demons are subject to us [by the power of] Thy Name!'' And
He said to them, ''I saw Satan fall like lightning from the
heavens. Behold, I have given you authority . . . over all the
enemy's powers, and nothing shall hurt you. Nevertheless,
do not rejoice in this, that the spirits are subject to you; rather
rejoice that your names are written in heaven.''

(Lk 10.17-20)

Firmly but gently, in dialogue and discourse, by means of parables
and personal example—as well as subtly, indirectly through the
teachings which He gives the populace, Jesus leads His disciples
on the path which they must follow:

Can a blind man lead a blind man? Will they both not fall
into a pit? A disciple is not above his teacher, but everyone
when he is fully taught will be like his teacher.
And why do you see only the speck which you perceive in
your brother's eye, yet you neglect to see the log that is ob-
vious in your own? . . . Why, you hypocrites! First remove
the log that obstructs your own vision and then will you be
able to see clearly enough to remove that speck which is in
your brother's eye.

(Lk 6.39-42)

He even enjoins His disciples to kill pride through humble self-
abasement in the service of others (ταπείνωσις). This swallowing
of ego, a favorite theme of the Psalmist and the Prophets, Jesus
makes a prerequisite for ministry. On the eve of the Passover, the
occasion of His own Passion and Death, He dramatically humbles
Himself at the feet of the disciples, even of Judas who was to betray
Him (Jn 13.3-17). Simon Peter, the proud fisherman, bridles at this
abasement of his ''Teacher and Lord,'' at first refusing to allow
Jesus to continue. But Jesus insists that the action is serious, for
''if I do not wash you, you have no part in Me,'' and at this Peter
profusely accepts His Lord's *diakonia*. It is one of the most profound incidents in the Gospel accounts.
All in all, Jesus repeatedly exercises his example to remind the
disciples of precisely the spirit His ministry entails them to abide by:

For I have given you an example, that you should do as I have done to you.

Truly, I tell you, a disciple is not above his teacher and a servant is not greater than his master. Nor is he greater than the one who sent him.

If you know these things, you are blessed if you act upon them and do them. . . .

(Mt 10.24, Jn 13.15-17)

Authority Rightly Dispensing the Word of Truth

The righteousness of the Kingdom, emphasizing above all repentance of the heart and positive turning to God (*metanoia*) in right praise, is what Jesus gives to His disciples as the true way of effectively reconciling fallen humanity. The saving act of the redeemed is that of response freely made, freely offered in cooperation (*synergia*) of will with God's own grace. Similarly must the disciples proceed, as dutiful Children of their Father in heaven and as servants of all.

This is in sharp contrast to what some of Jesus's contemporaries had defined and anticipated as the "righteousness" of the messianic Kingdom. Their emphasis was rather on the human fulfillment of the letter of the ancient Law, including the "traditions of the elders" which Jesus rejected as binding. Jesus saw such an emphasis as actually inhibiting the Evangel which Israel had to offer her own as well as the *oikoumene*.[24]

Always the faithful son of the Covenant, Jesus echoed the *Shema* of Deuteronomy, with which all faithful heirs of Israel begin their daily prayers. In doing so, He even put the Ten Commandments in perspective by insisting (as did the Prophets) on their integral meaning and application. The issue came to the fore during Jesus's dialogue with a zealous son of the Law:[25]

"Teacher, which is the first commandment of all? . . . What shall I do to inherit eternal life?" And Jesus said, "The foremost is, 'Hear, O Israel: The Lord our God is One.' . . . But what do you say, how is it written in the Law?"

And the man answered Him and said, "You are right, Teacher: you have said truly that He is One, and there is no other but He. To love Him with all the heart, and all the understanding, and all the strength one has, and likewise to love one's neighbor as oneself, is much more than all whole-burnt offerings and sacrifices."

And when Jesus saw that the man answered wisely, He said to him, "You are not far from the Kingdom of God: do this, and you will live."

After that, no one dared to challenge Him further.

Think not that I have come to abolish the Law and the Prophets. I have come not to abolish them, but to fulfill them. . . .

Truly I tell you, unless your righteousness exceeds that of the Scribes and Pharisees, you will never enter into the Kingdom of heaven.

It is not stretching the point to say that, by these teachings and the example of His ministry which demonstrated the practical implications of His Way, Jesus sorely challenged and shattered many of His contemporaries' conceptions both of the Law and the messianic Kingdom. In great measure, that is why He met death at the hands of the Roman and Jewish authorities, for all that He taught and did was "as one having authority."[26] His very choice of the Twelve "implied that the Messiah was here [neither as one] separated from His People [nor as one] to create one more group in Judaism beside those already existing," biblical theologian Veselin Kesich observes, "but to create a new community into which the People of Israel and the nations [alike] were called to enter, . . . a messianic community with the Messiah at its head."[27]

Jesus's last discourses this side of the grave were supreme acts of authority, compassion, and reconciliation, and they typically involved Yahweh and His Kingdom with real human persons who played a part in the scenario of His Life and Passion.

First, He proclaimed His own reconciliation in love and mercy, neither asking nor expecting reciprocity, with those who had rejected and persecuted His ministry. They had, in fact, brought Him to the climax of an apparently ignominious death on the hill of Golgotha, yet He sought even then to save them, not Himself:

"Father, forgive them, for they know not what they are doing!"(Lk 23.34).

Second, He took note of the unfortunate outcast and sinner who was suffering death on the cross beside Him. Hearing the man's words in His defense, He promised to reconcile Him to the Covenant of his fathers that very moment: "Truly I say to you, today you shall be with Me in Paradise" (Lk 23.39-43).

Lastly, the resurrection story is one of ultimate reconciliation. Jesus is the type of the "new Adam" who, in reconciling humankind to its Creator, has restored the power of life over death, righteousness over law and corruption, and faith, hope, and love over man's Promethean earthbound despair. The risen Jesus appeared to two disciples on the way to Emmaus (Lk 24.13-35) and, patiently enduring their nonrecognition, He soothed their aching hearts. "Beginning with Moses and all the Prophets, He explained to them all things in the Scriptures concerning Himself." Still they cannot see Who He is. Finally, when they came to the meal, "He took the bread and blessed and broke it, and gave it to them," and only then—in this familiar pastoral act of Eucharist—"their eyes were opened and they did recognize Him" as before. Jesus restored their faith and reconciled them to the ministry to which, only a few years before, He had called them.

The Great Commission: "Inescapably Evangelical and Ecumenical"

Just as "Jesus had received from God the authority needful for His work, so He conferred upon His followers the authority required for its continuance and extension"[28] as the Church— the Kingdom of God which has been inaugurated in the world to mediate the knowledge of Yahweh to all the world:

> Truly I tell you, freely you have received, [therefore] freely give. . . . He who receives anyone whom I send receives Me, and he who receives Me, receives Him Who sent Me.
> (Mt 10.8,14-15,40)
> Truly I tell you, whatever you bind on earth shall be bound in heaven, and whatever you loose on earth shall be loosed in heaven.

And again I tell you, if two of you agree on earth about anything they ask, it will be done by My Father in heaven. For where two or three are gathered in My Name, there am I in their midst.

(Mt 18.18-22)

Peace be with you. As the Father has sent Me, even so do I send you. . . . Receive the Holy Spirit. If you forgive the sins of any, they are forgiven; if you retain the sins of any, they are retained.

(Jn 20.19-23)

All authority in heaven and upon earth has been given to Me.

(Mt 28.18)

Go, therefore, into all the world and preach the Good News to the whole of creation (Mk 16.15). . . . Make disciples of all nations, baptizing them in the Name of the Father and of the Son and of the Holy Spirit, teaching them to observe all that I have commanded you. And, behold, I am with you always, to the close of the age.

(Mt 28.19)

With Jesus Christ, there is no distinction of persons or condition or background, whether saint or sinner. His is the pastoral theology of universal service and reconciliation, "inescapably evangelical and ecumenical," as Thomas Torrance argues. The Lord's Church, being that Body of His own which He has gathered and constituted out of the world as the New Covenant, must necessarily be "a reconciling as well as a reconciled community . . . sent by Christ into the divided world [in order] to find ways of overcoming disunity, so that the children of God everywhere may share in the unity of the creation restored in the Incarnation of the Word."[29]

NOTES

[1] Blaise Pascal, quoted in "The God of Abraham, Isaac, and Jacob in New Testament Theology"(Bo Reicke), *Unity and Diversity in New Testament Theology,* Robert A. Guelich, ed. (Grand Rapids, 1978), p. 186.

[2] Edwin Yamauchi, in "New Light on Gnosticism," *Christianity Today,* October 6, 1978, pp. 36-44. Also see: *ECF/B,* 10-12.

[3] *JBC* 77:118, 756.

[4] The celebrant's Prayer of Fulfillment, following the thanksgiving after Holy Communion, in the Divine Liturgy "according to the rites of our Father among the Saints, John Chrysostom of Constantinople," of the Eastern Orthodox Church.

[5] Saint Athanasios, *The Incarnation* 13.12, in *ECF/B,* p. 292.

[6] Ibid., *Exposition of Faith,* in *ECF/B,* 297.

[7] *Torah and Canon,* , pp. 54-59, 73-75. Also see: *JBC* 77:104-110, 754.

[8] Saint Athanasios, *Against Arius* 3.31-33, in *ECF/B,* 289-290.

[9] E.g., Mt 9.9-13/Mk 2.15-17/Lk 5.29-32: the story of the Lord's encounters and ministry to the "tax collectors and sinners (and) those who are sick, or in need of repentance." Also, Lk 19.1-10: Christ's encounter with Zaccheus, "for the Son of Man came to seek and save the lost."

[10] *JBC* 43:44, 71.

[11] *Love/N.T.,* pp. 51-52.

[12] Raymond E. Brown, S.S., in "The Last Discourse: xvii 9-26," *The Anchor Bible: The Gospel According to John, 29A* (Garden City, New York, 1970), pp. 758, 762, 766-68, 776.

[13] The word is also translated as "slave(s)."

[14] From the Commission proclamation introducing the "Prayer at the Ambon," in the Eastern Orthodox Liturgy.

[15] Mt 21.18-22. See also the hymns of the Matins "Bridegroom" Service of Monday of Holy Week, according to the observance of the Eastern Orthodox Church.

[16] *Love/N.T.,* pp. 142-43.

[17] Brown, "Last Discourse," pp. 776-77; *Love/N.T.,* p. 145; *JBC* 63.156, 457.

[18] Ibid., p. 769.

[19] *JBC* 63.155-56, 457.

[20] *Love/N.T.,* p. 145.

[21]*JBC* 63.156, 457.

[22]*G-EL/NT*, pp. 837-38.

[23]*JBC* 77.134-36, 78.17, 759, 772.

[24]See: Is 29.13; Mt 15.1-20/Mk 7.1-23; Mt 23 (esp. verse 15); Lk 11.37-41. Also: *JBC* 43.11, 64-65.

[25]See: Lev 18.5, 19.18; 1 Sam 15.22; Is 29.13; Hos 6.6; Mic 6.6-8; Mal 2.4-10,15,17; Mt 22.36-40/Mk 12.28-34/Lk 10.25-28; Mt 5.17,20.

[26]See: *CJC*, p. 14. Also: Dan 7.14; Mt 7.28-29, 26.63-65/Mk 14.61-64; Mk 2.27-28; Lk 4.32-37, 19.37-40; Jn 18.33-37.

[27]"Research and Prejudice," *Saint Vladimir's Theological Quarterly*, (1970), p. 43.

[28]*CJC*, p. 14. See also: Ceslaus Spicq, *Agape in the New Testament: Analysis of the Texts*, 3, Sisters M. A. McNamara and M. H. Richter, trans. (St. Louis, 1966), p. 45.

[29]Torrance, *Theology in Reconciliation: Essays Towards Evangelical and Catholic Unity in East and West* (Grand Rapids, 1976), p. 7.

The Church: Fulfilling the Covenant

In the view of the Orthodox Catholic Tradition, the Torah of
Israel, the Gospels of the Four Evangelists, and Acts and the
Epistles progressively reveal Yahweh's plan and story of the salvation of Israel and the nations. Cumulatively, they are the written
Word of God—Λόγος τοῦ Θεοῦ, theology in its most basic and
essential sense.[1] In the Law and the Prophets, Yahweh's universal lordship is revealed, then dims and is brought, at times un-
evenly, to the forefront of Israel's consciousness. In Christ, the
Gospels amplify and clearly proclaim the evangelical mission as
ecumenically imperative, according to the Lord Messiah's command, example, and consecration. The Acts and Epistles record
how the infant Church then developed and implemented Yahweh's
charter of salvation as a practical matter for all and amongst all.
In the Acts and Epistles, two key efforts stand out in bold relief:
first of all, the historic, watershed Council of Jerusalem which
brought to resolution the controversy over whether the Mosaic Law
and "traditions of the elders" would be binding anymore upon
Christians, Gentile converts in particular, and, secondly, the
outreach and reconciling ministry of Saint Paul, Apostle to the
Gentiles.

The Tension of the Law and the New Covenant

The Jewish/Gentile controversy was already an emerging theme
of concern as the following of Jesus expanded past Jerusalem and
Judea and outside the traditional confines of the Jewish synagogue
in the diaspora. It surfaced initially as a crucial issue with the conversion of the Roman centurion, Cornelius. The Apostles Peter and
Paul were drawn directly into the heart of the dispute, beginning—
we are told in Acts 10—with heavenly visions to Cornelius and to
Peter himself.

"A devout, God-fearing man [who] was praying to God unceas-
ingly, Cornelius saw in a vision . . . an angel of God coming within
himself." The angel reassured the conscientious Roman that,

although not a Jew, he and his prayers and good works were fully
acceptable "for a memorial before God," and he was instructed
to seek out Peter. Meanwhile, Peter had experienced a similar vision. The Great Commission of Christ and the events of Pentecost,
the Apostle was instructed, had brought to fulfillment the day when
the God-fearing among the Gentiles no longer needed to be cir-
cumcised; they were to be received on the merits, in Christ, of their
actual faith and good works as People of the Covenant and co-
heirs with Israel in the Kingdom. To the mixed assembly comprising
Cornelius and his household and a delegation of Jewish Christians,
Peter announced this news:

> You yourselves know how unlawful it is for a Jew to
> associate with a Gentile or to visit him. Yet God has shown
> me that I should call no one unholy or unclean.
> Therefore, I come as summoned, no longer contesting it
> or reluctant. . . . For truly I perceive that God is not one to
> have favorites, but that in every nation the person who fears
> God and does what is righteous is the one who is acceptable
> and is welcome to Him.
>
> (Acts 10.28-29,34-35)

Those who had joined with Peter for the encounter with Cornelius were astonished at the Apostle's words. Their astonish-
ment, however, changed to acceptance when, in the course of the
prayerful dialogue, "the gift of the Holy Spirit was poured out
upon the Gentiles, too" (Acts 10.44-45). As a result, Peter proceeded
to baptize Cornelius, together with all his family and household,
incorporating them within the Covenant community. At least in
recorded history, this was the first time in the infant Church's experience when Gentile proselytes were accepted without having
to conform to rigorous observance of the Mosaic Law and traditions.

It is easy to perceive why this unprecedented action left Peter
and his party open to criticism, especially—the Acts 11 account
observes—among "the Apostles and brethren throughout Judea."
The latter's normal empathy towards the ways of the Torah was
one factor; but, regardless of their inclinations one way or the other,

they were also apprehensive about the reaction of the Jewish authorities, who were harassing them as antinomian apostates. When the Judeans confronted Peter, he recounted his vision once more, how he had been instructed and fed by the Lord and how the Holy Spirit of God had favored Cornelius and his household. Concluding his defense of the actions that he and his brethren had undertaken, Peter said:

> And I remembered the word of the Lord, . . . that you be baptized in the Holy Spirit.
>
> If, therefore, God gave to [these Gentiles] the same gifts as He gave to us [in the Pentecost], upon believing in the Lord Jesus Christ, who was I to be able to stand in the way of God's own will?
>
> (Acts 11.16-17)

The disciples present offered no further challenge and, instead, "glorified God, saying, 'then surely God has granted to the Gentiles the same repentance and conversion [as ourselves]'" (Acts 11.18).

In a still very transitional, fledgling community, however, this did not and could not end the controversy then and there. For one thing, it is unlikely that word of these developments had actually become known to the scattered whole. "A great famine occurred throughout all the world," and King Herod Agrippa and the Jewish authorities had mounted fresh persecutions of the Christians (Acts 11.28, 12.1ff). The attention of the majority was, understandably, directed toward survival, mutual relief efforts, and evangelism outside Judea.

Acts 15 informs us that, either in opposition to the reception of the Gentiles outside of the Mosaic prescriptions or possibly even in ignorance of it, "certain men from Judea . . . of the sect of the Pharisees" began insisting upon circumcision and total enforcement of the Torah tradition as prerequisites for Baptism as Christians. The events now became a matter of community-wide concern and relevance, and some definitive action was called for.

Confident of the Holy Spirit's guidance when, in faith and

conscious of the need of the Church, they might undertake common council among themselves (Mt 18.18-22), "the Apostles and
presbyters" of the young Church assembled in Jerusalem to air
the question fully, consult together, and render a conciliar decision. "When there had been much disputing back and forth"
among the leadership present, Peter arose to reiterate his earlier
witness. Again, he informed the assembly of what his experience
had been:

> God made a choice among you, that years ago through my
> witness[2] the Gentiles should hear the Word of the Gospel
> and come to believe. And God . . . put no difference between
> us and them, cleansing their hearts by faith, even as He did
> with us.
>
> Now why, therefore, do you tempt God, trying to fasten
> a yoke upon the neck of the disciples, a requirement which
> neither our forefathers nor we ourselves were able to bear?
> Rather we believe that, through the grace of the Lord Jesus
> Christ, we shall truly be saved, and in the same way, so the
> Gentiles as well.
>
> (Acts 15.7-11)

Similar testimony was also given by co-workers Barnabas and Paul.
It was the traditionalist James, head of the pivotal Jerusalem Church
and the president of the council, who proposed the basic solution
which the conferees adopted:

> The Apostles and presbyters and brethren send greeting
> unto the brethren of the Gentiles in Antioch and Syria and
> Cilicia:
>
> It seemed good to the Holy Spirit, and to us, to lay upon
> you no greater burden than these necessary things: to ab-
> stain from meats sacrificed to idols, from blood, from things
> that have been strangled, and from fornication. If you keep
> yourselves free from such practices, you do well enough. May
> you fare well!
>
> (Acts 15.23-29)

After the Lord's Great Commission, this decree constituted the first universal canon for the Church ecumenical. Its effort was to affirm as the norm what had earlier been perceived as, at best, a measure of "economy," undertaken under extraordinary authority to address a particular pastoral problem. Yet, by most accounts, a genuine Jewish/Gentile diversity persisted within the whole expression of the Church, at least until after the fall of Jerusalem (A.D. 70) and the "Great Sanhedrin" Council of Jamnia (A.D. 100), which canonized for centuries to come official Judaism's anathema against Christianity.[3]

The question naturally arises: in the wake of the Jerusalem council's consensus, what was the dominant Christian leadership's attitude toward diversity and especially in regard to the Torah-oriented communities of the New Covenant? Was there a conscious, underlying effort to draw a pronounced line of demarcation between the New Covenant and Torah, and, therefore, gradually to write out of existence those communities which synthesized both observances equally as Jews and Christians? There is, however, no historical evidence that this was the case.

In the first place, James and the presbyters of the Jerusalem Church testified proudly of how faithful Jews of the time had accepted Jesus as the promised Messiah, in the context of His New Covenant authority, and retained their integrity as sons and daughters of the House of Israel:

> You see, brethren, how many thousands there are among the Jews of those who have believed [and yet] are zealots for the Law.
>
> (Acts 21.20)

A second key example is Paul, the converted Nazarite and Pharisee who—by his own testimony and other accounts—followed the Torah observances in his spiritual life upon every occasion possible.[4] In his relations with Judaism *per se,* as well as with his traditionalist Jewish Christian brethren, the Apostle to the Gentiles felt that a breach of that fellowship would frustrate his ministry, meaning that he had "run in vain" (Gal 2.2).[5] No doubt, as can be

seen in his defense against his former compatriots' charges that
he had betrayed Temple and Torah—even leading other good Jews
to violate the ancient Covenant,[6] Paul is deeply conscious of the
umbilical ties and the need to maintain "organic continuity with
Israel together with the opening out of Israel into the coming
oikoumene."[7] To "sunder that organic bond" could only maim
the Church and synagogue communities alike, "for each suffers
mutilation in separation from the other."[8]

Numerous examples abound of Paul's caution in this regard.
It was "Paul's customary practice" (Acts 17.2), in virtually all his
visits to the cities and villages in Judea and the diaspora, to observe
the pieties of the Law. As did his Jewish brethren of strict observance, he prayed and kept the Sabbath and, as a visiting rabbi,
taught in the Temple and the synagogues.[9] Furthermore, in Acts
there are two revealing incidents of Paul's meticulous concern in
this regard:

> [In Lystra] he found a disciple named Timothy, the son
> of a Jewish Christian mother and a Gentile father. As
> [Timothy] was well spoken of, . . . Paul wanted to have him
> in his company before departing. So he took [Timothy] and
> circumcised him, out of consideration for the Jews who
> dwelled in that district. . . .[10]
>
> (Acts 16.3)

> In conformance to the Law, . . . Paul took the [Nazarites]
> and the next day purified himself along with them, and went
> into the Temple, giving notice of the completion of the days
> of Purification, until the sacrifice was offered for each.
>
> (Acts 21.20-26)

Yet—as the zealous evangelist for the Messiah's New Covenant—
this same devoted son of Torah viewed circumcision "according
to the flesh" as unnecessary. He termed the canons of the Torah
and its Temple's bloody sacrifices as inadequate, and possibly even
constituting an actual barrier to Yahweh's Covenant for the salvation of individual persons and of humankind as a whole.

The two sides of the one Paul are not irreconcilable, however. Simultaneously the "Hebrew of the Hebrews, in attitude to the Law, a Pharisee" (Phil 3.5-6) and "Apostle of the Gentiles" (Rom 11.13), Paul, like his Lord, saw the practice of the Law among many of his coreligionists "mutilated" (Phil 3.2-3); it had become more of a fetish than an instrument of Yahweh's saving Covenant. He sought to keep everything in perspective, exercising "moderation [in all] to all" (Phil 4.5). He was mindful, as a steward of the Church, of the need "to build up, not tear down, consonant with the authority which the Lord has given me" (2 Cor 13.10). For him, this economy in encountering others and in managing the Lord's vineyard "in truth" was a *sine qua non,* especially in regard to being sensitive to the diversity of human experience and people's needs. If the refusal either to practice or to set aside these types of observance, according to particular circumstances, would create a "stumbling block" to the saving work of his Lord's Gospel, then he (or any other Christian leader) would some day have to answer to God Himself for it:

> Woe is me, if I do not preach the Gospel. . . . In order that I may win all the more to the Gospel, I have made myself servant of all.
> To the Jews, I became as a Jew, that I might win the Jews; to those under the Law, as one bound by the Law, although I was not bound to the Law, in order that I might win [for Christ] those who are under the Law. . . .
> (1 Cor 9.16,19-20)

Economy and moderation do not produce duplicity or timidity. But for the hard-core Judaizers, both economy and moderation were anathema. If they are not boldly and honestly confronted, Paul observes, their "all-or-nothing" mentality can lead to distrust and schism in the very fellowship of the Church. The ultimate, unhappy result would be the compromising of the Saviour's Great Commission to "witness [to the Gospel] in the remotest parts of the earth [and] make disciples of all nations."[11] The Way of Jesus Christ, the Church, would be reduced to no more than a particular type of messianic ethical school and denominational sect of Judaism, instead of becoming its fulfillment as the Lord Jesus had promised.

This is Paul's argument as he confronted others in the Church's leadership. The issue was now involving the growing Gentile mainstream and would ill serve the Church as a whole, he notes in his Epistle to the Galatians (2.11ff).[12] He severely reproaches Peter, James, and even his beloved co-worker Barnabas for behaving with a double standard, for giving false witness to the Gospel:

> When Peter came to Antioch, I had to confront him to his face, because he had done things for which rightly is he to be condemned.
>
> The story is this: before the coming of certain [Judaizers] from [the household of] James, Peter would always eat with Gentiles. But when those persons came, he took care to separate himself [from the company of the Gentile Christians] because he feared the circumcisers.
>
> The rest of the [Christian] Jews there also joined him in this act of hypocrisy. Even Barnabas was misled.

The Gospel of Christ is ecumenical. Ultimately, none of the distinctions of this world can bar or inhibit salvation for "Jew or Gentile, slave or freeman, male or female, for all are one in Christ Jesus . . . heirs according to [Yahweh's] promise" (Gal 3.28-29). Salvation is God's free gift (Rom 4.16). As such, it can neither be inherited by virtue of ethnic lineage nor earned by mere observance of law or performance of good works alone. Salvation of all is inherent in the very order of God's creation:

> For the anxious longing of all creation awaits in eager anticipation for the revelation of the sons of God, . . . groaning and travailing in pain as one, until now.
>
> (Rom 8.19,22)

What part can the disciples of the Messiah possibly have with those who would limit salvation or inhibit the unity of God's People?

Heresy, Heretics, and the Church's Unity

For Paul, it is not diversity which is the threat to the Church as that fellowship of peace, love, and right praise "in spirit and truth" which is Yahweh's "uniting bond of perfect completion" (Eph 4.3, Col 3.14). Diversity can and should exist in proliferation in a Church which embraces the *oikoumene* in piety, practice, forms, and even teachings which are complementary within the whole. Such diversity will, as a faithful icon, reflect the true conditions and needs of those persons, families, and communities which constitute humankind as God's holy creation.

On the contrary, the threat Paul perceives is one of heresy and heretics, doctrines and persons which act to "teach perversely" and distort the realities of God and creation (Acts 20.29). Some such as the Gnostics, involve "fables and endless genealogies" (1 Tim 1.4) and induce speculation in place of solid faith and loving fellowship. Others, like the hard-core Judaizers, engage in "contentions and strivings about the Law," offering stones to a spiritually hungry humankind rather than "the economy of God which builds up and instructs in faith" (Tit 3.9, 1 Tim 1.4).

When the Apostle uses the terms heresy and heretics, it is not primarily in the sense, respectively, of a proposition of false gods and cosmologies or of those who believe and teach heterodox creeds. His is an enmity directed against their new effect: seducing the disciples, "scandalizing the little ones" away from the "one Lord, one Faith, one Baptism" in which the Church of Christ is constituted (Mt 18.6-14,Lk 17.1-2; Eph 4-5). Their root sin is one of offending against the unity of the Body of Christ. Αἵρεσις and αἱρετικός are falsehoods that foster factions and division among those who are joined in the Covenant, lies that mutilate and break the branches of the Vine which sustains, and arterial blockages that prevent the particular joints or members of the Body from receiving the Blood of Life freely.[13] This image of the essential unity of Christ and His Church, constituted as one in truth and love, is the key to the Pauline theology:

Speaking the truth in love, we are to grow up in every way, in all things unto Him Who is the Head, into Christ from Whom the whole Body is fitly joined and covenanted together by those gifts which each of the individual joints supplies, according to the measure and ability of each part. This makes for the building up of itself in love. . . .

Put away the lie. Speak the truth, each one to his neighbor, for truly are we members one of the other.

(Eph 4.15-16,25)

As one leading participant of today's ecumenical movement has observed, the witness of the Holy Scriptures—especially of Saint Paul—is that "disunity, caused only by human vanity" is "an act of treason and betrayal of Christ, and of our very soul."[14] Archbishop Iakovos comments that Saint Paul voiced his dismay over it "in a soul-shaking and caustic manner":

Now I am begging you, brothers and sisters, through the Name of our Lord Jesus Christ: agree among yourselves, let there be no divisons and factions among you. Rather, be you all united in the same mind, joined together in the self-same judgment.

For, mind you, I have been informed by Chloe's household, my brothers and sisers, that there are indeed strifes and contentions among you. I hear that each of you is choosing sides, saying: I am of [the party of] Paul, and I of Apollos, and I of Cephas, and I of Christ.

How can this be, tell me? Is Christ, then, divided? Who was crucified for you? Certainly not Paul! Were you somehow baptized in the name of Paul? . . .

Is it not written, "I will destroy the wisdom of the wise and sophisticated, and I will bring to nothing and set aside the understanding of those perceived by this world as prudent. . . ." Has not God made foolish the wisdom of this world [in order] that no flesh may boast in its own right in His presence? By His doing, you are in Christ Jesus, Who became for us the Wisdom that is from God, the righteousness and holiness and very deliverance unto freedom.

This is true. As the Scriptures say, Let the one who wants to boast, glory only in the Lord. That glory is sufficient [to any].

(1 Cor 1.10-13,19,20,29-31)

Saint Paul perceived a divisive spirit, not sincere convictions held according to one's mind and heart, as the basic source of heresy and heretics. It is the fruit of selfish human vanity, an act of rebellion against God and His Covenant, Paul sternly warned his disciple Titus:

Rebuke heretics severely, in order that they may come to their senses and return to the health [of the one Body] in faith.

Speak, exhort, and reprove them in exercise of your godly authority. But if after the first and second admonition they still persist, reject and avoid them."

(Tit 1.13, 2.15, 3.10)

Paul as Conciliator

The man of frank confrontation and admonition of heretics in the interest of unity is likewise the man of reconciliation in the interest of that same unity. That quality, in Greek καταλλαγή, is Paul's favorite word for the essence of Christian discipleship, echoing his Lord's own teaching that it is the bringing of peace to one another and to all that makes the disciples "the salt which gives savor to the earth" (Mk 9.50).

Paul then goes a significant step further. The true worshipper, as Jesus says, may only approach Yahweh's holy Altar by becoming reconciled in peace with the other (Mt 5.24). Moving beyond the Old Testament and intertestamental perspective of a relatively passive process of reconciliation, Paul heightens the notion considerably.[15] He emphasizes both a participatory act of reconciliation and an understanding of Jesus Christ as supremely the subject Who is seeking to reconcile and to be reconciled. Alike this activist conciliatory role belongs to all disciples of Jesus, who are themselves "other Christs" by virtue of their baptism (Gal 3.27, Col 3.10-12):

> Therefore, if any person be in Christ, it is a new creation. The old ways are now passed away, and yet, behold, they have become new.
>
> All things are of God, who, having reconciled (καταλ-λάξαντος) us to Himself through Christ, has given unto us the ministry of reconciliation (καταλλαγῆς).
>
> Thus God was in Christ, reconciling (καταλλάσσων) the world unto Himself, not counting their trespasses against them. He has commissioned us to [carry out] this word[16] of reconciliation (τόν λόγον τῆς καταλλαγῆς).
>
> (2 Cor 5.17-19)

A reconciliation that calls for "not counting their trespasses against them" is one that, just as Yahweh has done, must go far beyond simple forgiveness or the act of overlooking another's offenses, past or present. This New Covenant understanding of reconciliation seeks to implement the Saviour's own admonition (Mt 5.41-42, Lk 6.30) to go "the extra mile, . . . not to refuse the one who begs, or who would borrow from you." In that manner, it becomes an act which "exceeds the virtue of the Scribes and Pharisees," whose concept was more one of obligation.

> By virtue of this, we ourselves are ambassadors in behalf of Christ. Indeed, God is beseeching through us. Now we, in behalf of Christ, beg that you yourselves be reconciled to God (καταλλάγητε τῷ Θεῷ).
>
> (2 Cor 5.20)

> For while we were yet enemies,[17] we were reconciled (κα-ταλλάγημεν) to God through the Death of His Son. Now, having been reconciled (καταλλαγέντες), even more shall we be saved through His Life.
>
> And not only this, but we are also rejoicing in God through our Lord Jesus Christ, by Whom we have received

(τήν καταλλαγήν ἐλάβωμεν).

(Rom 5.10-11)

Even with so activist an emphasis on the meaning and implications of reconciliation, Paul does not seem quite satisfied. According to the interpretation of some commentators,[18] in order to express the theme more emphatically, he appears to have coined a new combination word and usage—ἀποκαταλλάσσω. It is apparently intended and understood as an analogy to ἀποκαθίστημι (noun ἀποκατάστασις), signifying both a restoration of things to their former, better state of being as well as "the renewal of a new and better era."[19]

As "Abba, our Father," Yahweh is the all-Merciful and He offers to all of humankind complete restoration to His favor—to and even beyond that ideal, wholistic relationship and state of being, which the primeval Adam enjoyed in the state of Paradise. This promise is extended as well to those who are "afar off":

> But now in Christ Jesus, you who were afar off were brought near by the Blood of Christ.
>
> For He is our peace, the One Who has made both as one, having broken down the enmity [of old], that middle wall that had made for separation between us. . . in order that He might reconcile (ἀποκαταλλάξη) both, restoring both to God's favor as one Body through the cross. By that cross, in fact, He has put to death that enmity which had been. . . .

(Eph 2.13-16)

The elaboration of the theme directly evokes the language and spirit of the Old Testament Prophets, especially, again, in the ecumenical outreach to the Gentiles, who have been until this time "afar off" from the Covenant (Is 44.5, 56.7-8; Zeph 3.9). All, as the covenanted disciples of the Messiah, are "no longer servants, . . . but friends" (Jn 15.14-16). Nor any longer are they to be regarded and treated as "strangers and foreigners, but rather fellow citizens with the saints, even of the household of God . . .

constituted upon the foundation of the Apostles and Prophets, Jesus Christ being the very cornerstone" (Eph 2.19-20). It is through Jesus that those who formerly pitched their tents in opposing camps, Gentiles and Jews, are to be reconciled "by the Spirit to the Father [as] a holy Temple, a place where God's Spirit dwells within" (Eph 2.18,21-22).

There is no exclusivity operating here. The disciples of Christ, Paul teaches, must take care to discover the incarnate Word of God and His Spirit in "whatever is true and righteous, whatever is honorable and pure and beautiful, whatever comes of good report, just so it be virtuous and praiseworthy" (Phil 4.8). The works of God in the ancient Torah of Israel, Yahweh's original Chosen, are to be reconciled with "the altars [of God-fearing Gentiles] to an unknown God" which Paul and successive generations of disciples would discern in the wider *oikoumene*.

It is not necessarily the origin or character, or even in some cases the motives, of the particular agency which determines the effectiveness or validity of the proclamation of the Word of God.[20] It is the kerygma itself, for "the important thing is that in every way, whether in pretense or in truth, Christ is proclaimed, . . . strengthening the hands that are weak and the knees that are feeble, and healing the limb that is lame" (Phil 1.17-18, Heb 12.12-13).

The disciple of Christ, then, "must go the extra mile" (Mt 5.41) to reconcile and unify, always trying to keep open the lines of communication. Only reluctantly, in extreme situations where he finds a "breaking of faith" in the teaching and doing of scandal and heresy must he sever the bond which, however tenuously, might maintain the communion or at least offer prospects of reconciliation in Christ.

Shepherds and Servants in Discipleship

The image of Lord and disciple as Good Shepherd, discerning and compassionate both for those within the flock and for those who have been lost or straying, is articulated particularly in the Evangelists' stories of Jesus's ministry and that which He intends for those who would take up His "sweet yoke" of discipleship.

He engaged repeatedly in earnest, person-to-person dialogue with Sanhedrin officials and zealous students of the Torah, "for months reasoning together with them in the synagogue every Sabbath, trying to persuade Jews and Greeks alike . . . about the Kingdom of God" (Acts 18.4,19ff & 19.8). Meeting the self-assured Epicurean and Stoic philosophers of Athens on their own home ground, he even quoted back to them their own poets, "in order that they should seek God and, perhaps, in groping for Him be able finally to discover Him—though, truthfully, He is not far from any one of us." Although not always apparently fruitful, for Paul it was enough that the Word was proclaimed and "some persons did join him and believed" (Acts 17.16-34).

If some still fear the enterprise, or hold back stingily of their resources in entering into the fray, Paul reminds them of the Lord's warning that they rightly earn scorn as "wicked and slothful servants" who will be unable to "enter into the joy of the Lord" (Mt 25.14-30, Lk 19.11-27). That this is not a hypothetical concern Paul evidences by his admonition to the Christians at Corinth:

> He who sows sparingly shall likewise reap sparingly. He who sows bountifully shall likewise reap bountifully, with blessings to spare. . . . There should be no reluctance, nor forced enthusiasm, for it is the cheerful giver whom God loves.
> (2 Cor 9.6-7)

O ye of little faith! Do you torture yourself that you will be inadequate to future tasks?[23] The Lord has encouraged us, he says, "not to be anxious for [our] life," but to trust that our Father in heaven "knows full well that you need all of these things" (Mt 6.25-34). In the final analysis, Paul says, He will provide according to our own needs:

> For it is in God's power to provide all grace in abundance to you, so that having always sufficiency in all, you will be able amply to meet each and every situation and to provide for every good cause. . . . He who supplies seed to the sower and bread for food will supply your seed for sowing and the

harvest of your righteousness many times over. . . .

(2 Cor 9.8-11)

When some Corinthians felt that they had to draw the line somewhere in their associations and outreach, if only for the sake of their own and the Church's reputation, Paul gently suggested that they were in danger of succumbing to fear and sectarian self-righteousness:[24]

> Let no one seek his own good, but instead that of his neighbor. Eat anything that is sold in the meat market, without making inquiries . . . for "the earth is the Lord's and all that it contains."
>
> And if one of the unbelievers invites you, and you wish to go, eat anything that is set before you, again without making inquiries for conscience's sake. . . .
>
> Whether, then, you eat or drink or whatever you do, do all to the glory of God.
>
> Give no offense, do not push away Jews or Gentiles or those of the Church of God itself; in the same way I also please all persons in all things, not to seek my own profit, but the increase of the many, that they may be saved.
>
> Be imitators of me, just as I am of Christ.
>
> (1 Cor 10.24-33, 11.1)

Others in the same community confronted Paul with his instructions on another occasion on associating with immoral people, to which he replied:

> Yes, I wrote to you in my letter not to associate with immoral people. But by no means did I intend for you not to associate with the immoral people of this world, or with those who covet and swindle, or with idolaters. If you did that, you would have to leave this world completely!
>
> Actually, I meant for you to shun any person among the brethren, if he should be . . . such a one.
>
> After all, what have I to do with judging those who are

not of the faithful? Do you not take care to discipline those
who are within the Church?

As for those outside, they are for God to judge. You be
concerned to remove the wicked ones from among your own
company.

(1 Cor 5.9-13)

In other words, discipleship by its very nature calls for an outreach
and open spirit of association that is realistic in its assessment of
the world in which we live. There can be no single, rigid "rule
of thumb" in meeting these diverse situations and types of people. Nevertheless, the Apostle does call unequivocally here for order
and moral code—and pastoral institutions of godly discipline—to
be applied within the Body of believers.

One Lord, One Faith, One Baptism . . . Yet, Many Diverse Gifts

On the other hand, the Apostles and disciples had no illusions
that a complete, true sharing of fellowship was easily to be achieved.
There is among the faithful a unity of Sacrament and discipleship,
a commonality of sacred identity that can be entered into only in
the confession and sharing of the same sacred Faith—that is, in
the Way, the Truth, and the Life of Jesus Christ and the Church
which He constituted in fulfillment of the Covenant:

Thus we who are many are one Body in Christ, members
one of the others.

(Rom 12.5)

Our Lord Jesus Christ . . . is the head of the Body, the
Church [in that] it pleased the Father that in Him all fullness
should dwell . . . continue truly in the Faith, firmly established and steadfast, not moved away from that hope which
is the Gospel you have heard.

(Col 1.18-23)

Come, let yourselves be built as living stones, into one
spiritual Temple, . . . to offer spiritual sacrifices acceptable
to God through Jesus Christ. . . .

> You are a Chosen People, a royal priesthood, a holy nation . . . whom God has claimed for His very own, to show forth and proclaim rightly the praises of Him who has called you out of darkness into His marvelous light. You are now God's People.
>
> (1 Pet 2.5,9)

> He has made us to be a kingdom, priests before God the Father, . . . to reign upon the earth.
>
> (Rev 1.6, 5.10)

In the apostolic view, then, it is a contradiction in terms for the faithful to be "yoked together unnaturally (ἑτεροζηγοῦντες) as one to the unfaithful, the unbelievers."[25]

> What kind of fellowship can there be between rightousness and lawless unrighteousness? What communion has light with its absence? What concord does Christ have with demonic worthlessness? How can the one who believes partake with the one who does not believe? Where can there be union between God's Temple and the false gods? For you and I are shrines, the Temple of the living God.
>
> (2 Cor 6.14-16)

We find similar admonitions in Eph 5.5-17, as well as in the three Johannine Epistles (1 Jn 2.15, 2 Jn 8-11, 3 Jn 11).[26] Paul tells his eager, but perhaps susceptible community of converts in Thessalonike that they must be careful, in the face of all sorts of false prophets and disbelievers, to "hold fast to the traditions [of the Gospel]" which they had learned from his instruction and letters (2 Thes 2.15).

It is equally important "not to quench the Spirit nor to despise [different] prophetic gifts" in the life of the Church. It is often easy to confuse essentials of faith and covenant with matters which are secondary or vary according to different circumstances. To do so is to deify the man-made "traditions of the elders," that is, akin to the "virtue of the Scribes and Pharisees" above which the Lord Jesus has insisted His disciples must rise. The Church's leaders and members, therefore, must "examine everything carefully, and take hold of that which is good" (1 Thes 5.19-22).

No two persons, families, communities, or cultures are alike. That was the primary lesson of the historic Council of Jerusalem. A body uniform in all its particulars would not be authentic, as the Church is called to incarnate the Word of God amidst the reality of humankind; she must reflect, as a faithful icon, the very diversity of persons existing within the Triune God. We are compelled to recognize that:

> . . . there are varieties of gifts, but the same Spirit . . . varieties of ministries, yet the same Lord . . . varieties of operation, yet it is the same God Who works all things in all.
>
> Thus to each one is given the [particular] manifestation of the Spirit that is most suitable to that person for effecting the common good . . . one and the same Spirit is at work in all these things, distributing to each one individually just as He wills. . . .
>
> For even as the body is one and yet has many members, and all the members of the body, though many and diverse, nevertheless constitute one body, so also is Christ. . . .
>
> For the body is not one member, but many. . . .
>
> God has placed the members, each one of them, in the body, in just such as He desired. For if they were all one member, where would the body be? But, in fact, there are many members, but one Body . . . Christ's Body, of which you are individually members.
>
> (1 Cor 12)

Pressing home essentially the same point, Peter puts the emphasis on the value of the various persons and their gifts as serving one another and hearing well what the other has to say:

As each one has received a special gift, employ it in serving one another, as good stewards of the manifold grace of
God.

Whoever speaks, let him speak . . . whoever serves, let him
do so as by the strength which God alone supplies, so that
in all things God may be glorified through Jesus the Messiah,
to Whom belongs the glory and dominion, forever and ever.
Amen.

(1 Pet 4.10-11)

The Eucharistic Fellowship of the Faithful

What is it that unites these diverse gifts, ministries, operations,
and prophecies in "effecting the common good" and "serving one
another" as members of the one Body which is Christ and His
Church? As the Lord Jesus, in fulfillment of the Torah, taught His
disciples and the young lawyer, the unity is found in the Great
Commandment of love. When all else perishes, "faith, hope, and
love remain, but the greatest and most enduring among these is
love" (1 Cor 12).

The sign of love's enduring reality, effected within the fellowship
of the one Church, is that which completes the "one Faith" and
"one Baptism": the faithful in assembly together as one, immersed
in holy *anamnesis* (living enactment and remembrance) of Christ
the Lord and sharing in *Eucharistia* (right thanksgiving) of the
holy Supper which He gave us. All who fully share in the "one
Faith" and "one Baptism" without adulteration are called to com-
mune as one in this shared Eucharistic supper of fellowship,
established explicitly by Divine ordinance.[27] As the "reasonable,
logical and bloodless worship" given to and commanded for all,[28]
the Eucharist is the Liturgy (*Leitourgia*—ἔργα τοῦ Λαοῦ) of the
People of God which is "explicitly characterized as a means to
unity" and concelebrated therein "as a means of continual renewal
and strengthening of their unity" as the Church:[29]

The Cup of blessing which we bless, is it not the Communion of the Blood of Christ? The Bread which we break, is

it not the Communion of the Body of Christ? For we being many are one Bread, one Body, for we are all partakers of that one Bread. . . .

You cannot be partakers of the Lord's Table and of the table of demons alike. . . .

For I have delivered to you what I received from the Lord, namely, that the Lord Jesus, on that same night in which He was betrayed, took bread:

And when He had given thanks, He broke it, and said, "Take, eat: this is My Body, which is broken for you. Do this in remembrance of Me."

And in the same manner He also took the Cup, when He had supped, saying, "This Cup is the New Covenant in My Blood. Do this yourselves, as often as you drink it, in remembrance of Me."

For as often as you eat this Bread, and drink this Cup, you do manifest and proclaim the Lord's [redemptive] Death until He comes.

(1 Cor 10.16-17,21; 11.23-26)

Paul felt that he had to remind the wayward, fractious Corinthian community of the explicit nature and elementary facts of the Lord's Supper, because they "no longer partook of the common meal expressing their union with one another in the Lord, but each group ate apart."[30] They are denying something basic and essential to their fellowship in the Church, he warns them, and in doing so they give the lie to the true Presence of the Lord in the midst of each and every assembly of God's Church. They have taken a terrible sin on themselves, if they persist:

Wherefore, whoever shall eat this Bread and drink this Cup of the Lord unworthily shall be guilty and have to answer to the Lord for His Body and Blood. But let each one [truly] examine himself, and so let him eat of the Bread and drink of the Cup.

For the person who eats and drinks unworthily eats and

drinks damnation for himself, not discerning (that it is) indeed the Lord's Body.

(1 Cor 11.27-28)

If we attend closely to the particular context of the Apostle's
statements here, it is apparent that Paul sees the Corinthians' sin
as perhaps the most grievous of all. They have "missed the mark"
entirely and offend directly against the Lord's Great Commandment, which binds those who call themselves brethren of one
another and disciples of Jesus. For the sake of human vanity, they
have broken the organic bond of peace and love—among
themselves and with the Lord Himself.

To Paul, this raises the dreaded specter of disunity. It poses
the threat, moreover, of reducing the Lord's Supper to mere ritual
and empty symbolism, instead of true fellowship and godly
thanksgiving in the Lord's Body. Disparately observed in discord,
the very instrument and sign of unity becomes a cancer of heresy,
rendering null and void the working "in truth and love" of God's
Holy Spirit within the Church. This breaking of faith with Yahweh's
Covenant in the very Act of common prayer, profession of faith,
and breaking of bread together which is supposed to unite them
was to become both the primary reason for and the result of the
schisms in the history of the Church Ecumenical. It is, for that
reason, the hardest rent of all to repair in the "seamless robe of
Christ," in the view of the Churches of Catholic Orthodoxy.

Broken and distributed is the Lamb of God, broken yet never
sundered apart, eaten yet never consumed, making holy those
who partake truly. . . .

Lord, may the partaking of Thy holy Mystery be for me,
not for judgment or condemnation but for the healing of soul
and body.[31]

NOTES

[1]See Georges Florovsky, "The Lost Scriptural Mind" and "Revelation and Interpretation,"*Bible, Church, Tradition* (Belmont, 1972), pp. 9-36.

[2]I.e., to the Roman centurion and his household.

[3]F. F. Bruce, "James and the Church of Jerusalem,"*Peter, Stephen, James and John: Studies in Early Non-Pauline Christianity (Grand Rapids, 1979), pp. 86-119.*

[4]*Giuseppe Ricciotti, Paul the Apostle,* trans. Alba I. Zizzamia (Milwaukee, 1953): no. 280, 281, 282, pp. 218-20; no. 396, p. 307; Samuel Umen, *Links Between Judaism & Christianity* (New York, 1966), pp. 126, 140; W. D. Davies, "Introductions: Paul and Judaism since Schweitzer; Palestinian and Diaspora Judaism," *Paul and Rabbinic Judaism: Some Rabbinic Elements in Pauline Theology* (New York, 1967), pp. vii-xv, 1-16.

[5]Bruce, pp. 101ff. See also: *JBC* 49.16-17, pp. 239-240.

[6]Acts 13.16-41, 21.39, 22.3, 23.6, 26.5; Phil 3.5-6. See also: *JBC* 45.109, 46.13-14, pp. 210, 217-18.

[7]Torrance, *Theology in Reconciliation: Essays Towards Evangelical and Catholic Unity in East and West* (Grand Rapids, 1976), pp. 25-27.

[8]Ibid.

[9]E.g., Acts 13, 14.1, 17.2,10,17, 18.4, 19.8, 21.20-26; Rom 11.1, 2 Cor 11.22. See also: Ricciotti, nos. 331 & 332, pp. 260-61.

[10]Ricciotti, nos. 373 & 374, p. 292; Ronald Brownrigg, *Who's Who in the New Testament* (New York, 1971), p. 437.

[11]Mt 28.19/Mk 16.15/Jn 21.15-17/Acts 1.8.

[12]Panagiotis I. Bratsiotis, "The Apostle Paul and the Unity of the Church," *Orthodox Observer,* May 1961.

[13]*AGL,* p. 9; *G-EL/NT,* p.23. See also: Jn 15.1-11, Acts 20.29-30, 1 Cor 11.19, Gal 5.20, Phil 3.2, 2 Tim 4.3-4, and Tit 1.13, 2.15,3.10.

[14]Archbishop Iakovos, "The Unity of Christian Churches," *Orthodox Observer,* April 1961, a televised address to the New England region, Manchester, N.H., March 11, 1961.

[15]I. Howard Marshall, "The Meaning of Reconciliation," *Unity and Diversity in New Testament Theology* (Grand Rapids, 1978), pp. 117-32, ed. Robert A. Guelich.

[16]Understood as a transitive, i.e., active verb, reminiscent of patristic themes to the effect that "God is (active) verb," not the Deist's passive,

withdrawn deity.

[17]I.e., ensnared as participants in the thralldom of death, and, therefore inimical to life and God and under God's disfavor. See: ἐχθρός meaning, esp. in *G-EL/NT*, p. 331-Column B, and in *AGL*, p. 179, Column B. This is particularly indicated as the sense of ἐχθροί in view of the verses which immediately follow: Rom 5.12,14.

[18]Marshall, ibid.

[19]*AGL*, 42,43.

[20]*JBC*, 50.12, 249.

[21]Alphonse N. Didron, *Christian Iconography 1*, trans. E. J. Millington (New York, 1965), pp. 318-41.

[22]*JBC* 59.27, 60.2, 369-70, 378.

[23]*JBC* 52.31, 285.

[24]*JBC* 51.66-67, 269-70.

[25]*JBC* 52.24, 282-83.

[26]*JBC* 56.34-35, 348; *JBC* 62.15, 32, 34, 408, 412, 413. See also: Raymond E. Brown, *The Anchor Bible: The Gospel According to John*, 29A, (Garden City, N.Y., 1970), p. 778.

[27]Mt 26.26-29/Mk 14.12-25/Lk 22.15-20, and Jn 6.51-58.

[28]From the Prayers of Consecration of the Holy Gifts, in the Divine Liturgy of the Eastern Orthodox Church.

[29]Bratsiotis, "Apostle Paul."

[30]*JBC* 51.70-72, pp. 270-71; *Love/NT*, p. 139. See also: Leon Morris, *Testaments of Love: A Study of Love in the Bible* (Grand Rapids, 1981).

[31]Respectively, the celebrant's prayer of the Eucharistic Fraction and prayer of Preparation for Holy Communion, in the Divine Liturgy of the Eastern Orthodox Church.

CHAPTER FOUR:

Covenant and Pastoral Economy

The *consensus patrum,* the sum and synthesis of the pastoral acts and writings of the great Fathers and Ecumenical Synods of the Church,[1] witnesses to the Covenant which is recorded in the Holy Scriptures. However, the consensus is that the Covenant comes to be comprehended and effected "in spirit and truth," not in the act of reading or proclamation of the written Word *per se,*[2] but in acts of living remembrance by which Yahweh's "saving grace is revealed . . . to all of humankind."[3] Such revelation does not take place in the abstract, but in the context of this world in which we live. The Lord founded the Church as the worthy vessel through which His Word takes flesh. Dwelling in our midst, He performs the λογική λατρεία, the reasonable service[4] that is offered to the Father "in behalf of all and for all,"[5] and "grants knowledge in this world of His truth and everlasting life in the world to come."[6]

The "Magnificat," praise-hymn of the Theotokos, Saint Mary the Virgin Mother of our Lord, and the thank-hymn of Saint Zachariah, as found in the Gospel account of Saint Luke, together and succinctly affirm Orthodoxy's view of Yahweh's Covenant and pastoral economy in the mission of the Church:

> God our Saviour, Who is mighty above all, has compassionately regarded our lowly estate and has done great things. He spoke to our ancestors, to Abraham and thus to his descendants forever. By the voice of the Prophets, the Lord our God performs the mercy which He promised to our ancestors from all the ages.
>
> In living remembrance He keeps His holy Covenant with His People, to prepare His way and to give the knowledge of salvation to them, that they might live in holiness and righteousness throughout all their days and give light to those who dwell in darkness, in the shadow of death.[7]

In order to assure corporate unity and his Church's holy continuity

in "right praise," the Lord—by witness of the Scriptures[8] and
the life of His Church—has consecrated godly shepherds for His
flock. Their stewardship, as those anointed of the Lord, is to "rightly
discern the Word of Truth"[9] and to "administer all things to all
for the good, according to the needs of each and every one."[10]
It is "through that succession of continuity which flows from the
Apostles" that the charismata, the gifts of the Holy Spirit's abiding
pentecostal Presence, guarantee that "the Church may rightly and
in truth instruct, preserve our faith in the one God, and—without
danger of blaspheming God or dishonoring the Patriarchs and
Prophets—witness truly of the Scriptures."[11] Were it not for this
continuity and its assurance in the Lord, the Covenant recorded
in the Scriptures would "give way to as many different meanings
as there are people on earth"[12] and we would "transform the
kerygma [central message of God] into the mere word [of
man]."[13]

The great Cappadocian Father, Saint Gregory of Nyssa, saw
the Church's covenantal mission in terms of 2 Peter—of a redeemed
humankind being enabled to "reach out" in a process of continuing growth towards God's Kingdom[14] and thus to "become partakers of the divine nature" (1.4). The Church is the anteroom in
the Kingdom of God. In the eucharistic assembly, wherein the acts
of living remembrance come to fulfillment in the communion of
Saints, the Church is the chosen vessel for *gnosis,* that true comprehension of God which has now become available here on this
earth to every person and nation that desires to partake of His
life:

    Blessed are Thou, O Christ our God,
    Who made fishermen wise
      by sending upon them the Holy Spirit,
      and through them drew into Thy net
      the whole of the *oikoumene.* . . .
    Wherefore, with one voice
    we ever glorify
    the Spirit of God, the all-Holy.[15]

The Church is "one, holy, catholic, and apostolic"[16] precisely because she fulfills the messianic stewardship by the authority of the Holy Spirit,[17] Who, in the community of the blessed Trinity which is archetype of the Church, "proceeds from the Father."[18] The Church is the sacramental Body of Christ in this world and, as in His holy paschal sacrifice for that same world, may indeed be "broken, yet never sundered apart."[19] For the sake of her ecumenical mission, and despite divisions and misunderstandings of varying degrees, "the *Una Sancta* [has] never ceased to exist visibly."[20] This fact is essential to the Lord's mandate for His Church:

> [For] the nature of separation, when it concerns the Church, is as mysterious as the nature of unity itself.
>
> On the other side of the coin of the "mystery of union" is to be found the "mystery of disunion." God penetrates the wall of silence and manifests His real presence in the disunited parts of Christendom. Canonical illegitimacy does not bring with it invalidation of the reality itself; on both sides of the wall are to be found the same Body and the same Blood of the Saviour.
>
> This fact brings us to what may be called the negative (apophatic) aspect of unity. Negative (apophatic) theology and hesychastic tradition teach that the more ineffable God is in His nature, the more He can be experienced in His existence and His burning proximity. In the same way we may say . . . that the existing unity defies formulas, but in a certain sense it is evident and can be mystically experienced: at the most profound depth of her mystery, at the heart of her life, which is Christ, the Church remains one and undivided.[21]

"The Way of Life: To Make Peace Among Disputants"

At times the Church has taken a rather rigorist stance, known canonically as *akribeia,* with regard alike to those within the Body of the faithful as well as to those outside of her canonical communion. Thus does she "hold fast the Covenant" among the faithful and meet critical threats to her integrity.[22] But equally as often the Church exercises *oikonomia* of divine philanthropy. Respecting the twin mysteries of union and disunion, she has applied charity in the generous spirit of her Lord and set aside strict prescriptions for canonical rectitude, in the interest of the greater good to be served both within and outside of the Church's fold. Undoubtedly, this has led to some situations which, on the surface, appear to be illogical. For "the Eastern Church realized that logic was not always the happiest weapon to apply"[23] either to ecclesiastical disputes or, more generally, to those very human problems and conundrums which her pastors encounter so frequently in the life of the community. She has seen the need often to "cut the Gordian knot," rather than to undertake the often hopeless task of trying to unravel tangled situations:

> The Orthodox are more willing to join in the discussion so that there is hope that the outcome will be a true synthesis. . . . Though unchanging . . . and unyielding on doctrinal matters, the Orthodox can be surprisingly flexible on practical ones.
>
> In the early Church where there were many schisms and disputes in the East, the practice grew up that diocese A could be in communion with dioceses Y and Z, even though these latter two were not in communion with each other. . . . The fact is that in the early Church communion was not such an absolute and legalistic matter as it has become in later history. There were many cases of schism within a bishopric or between sees, but one broken link did not destroy the whole chain of unity.[24]

This is not contradiction. It is, rather, the paradox of the divine Body of Christ operating within the limitations and fallible condition of humankind, through the stewardship of His anointed shepherds.[25]

This economy in the Church's management of her household, as the Liturgy indicates, ultimately comes down to the root meaning of Orthodoxy: a rightly offered "mercy of peace and sacrifice of praise."[26] As the Way of Life in Christ, the Church is supremely God's agency in the world "to make peace among disputants"[27] and so reconcile all to their Creator. A brief historical review of the early Church's path in this way helps to illustrate the variety of approaches which she has applied in this task.

The Church early on gained the experience which has guided her ever since in this mission of reconciliation. Following the fall of Jerusalem to the Roman occupation in 70 A.D., the fledgling Christian communities were now anathema to their former brethren, the Jews of the Temple and the synagogue. The Apostles and the first generation of disciples were passing from the scene. Totally separated from their former brethren and, moreover, no longer considered to be a legitimate, protected denomination within Judaism, the Christians were now identified by the Roman authorities as an "atheistic" outlaw cult. This meant that no longer could they qualify for toleration under the "Jewish exception" from the official policy of the Empire, a policy which required that cultic veneration be rendered to the Emperor and his household gods.

Still in the process of establishing their own identity, some early Christians tended to look inward. This was the inclination especially of those who anticipated the final coming of Christ in His Kingdom, the *parousia*. They distrusted a world of conflicting values and lifestyles and saw its very being as an ever-present threat to their hopes for salvation. Others of Judaistic and Gnostic sectarian backgrounds or influences were inclined to view the world's manifestations and struggles as phantasms partaking of Satanic nature. Withal, it is no wonder that the attitude of some early Christians was, at best, aloof or nearly as exclusionary as that of the Essenes:

> If any clergyman or layperson shall be found to enter a synagogue of the Jews or of heretics, and in their company pray, let him be excommunicated. . . .
> And let any bishop or presbyter who accepts the Baptism

or sacrifice of any heretic as having validity be deposed, for what part does the believer have with the unbelieving?[28]

Even so, many other sober voices recalled that the New Covenant had the necessity to witness Christ and to carry out the Good News in service to all of humankind.[29] Unlike the Essenes, the early Church viewed the withdrawal into separate communities and ways of piety as a special prophetic call *only for some,* to lead a life in emulation of, for example, the Lord's Forerunner and kinsman, John the Baptist. But it was not the norm. The majority, though not of this world, were called to live *in* this world while following the way of Jesus and His disciples:

> Christians are not distinct from the rest of the people either in country or language or customs. For neither do they dwell anywhere in [special] cities of their own, nor do they use a different language, nor practice a conspicuous manner of life. . . . While they live in cities both Hellenic and barbarian, as falls to the lot of each, and follow the customs of the country in dress, food, and their general manner of life, they display the remarkable and assuredly surprising status of their citizenship.
>
> They live fully in the country of their heritage, but as sojourners, sharing all things as citizens, yet suffering as though they were foreigners. . . . Their lot is cast in this world, but they do not live for this world. They sojourn here on this earth, yet [viewing] their citizenship as in heaven. They obey established laws, while in their private lives they surpass these laws [in virtue]. They love all persons, yet are persecuted by all. . . .
>
> To put it briefly, what the soul is in the body, that the Christians are in the world.[30]

The common tie was the sharing community, living in the fellowship of agape as brothers and sisters who were following Christ in His Church. Whether of class, race, language, or customs and

former religious ties, the old barriers fell before the unifying force
of this ideal:

> We have a common fund, shared by every needy person.
> We who hated and killed one another [before] and, because
> of differing customs, would not even share a fireside, . . .
> now, following the Incarnation of Christ [in this world], live
> together as one.
> We pray for our enemies and try to persuade those who
> unjustly hate us that, if they will live according to the ex-
> cellent precepts of Christ, they, too, will have a good hope
> of receiving the same reward as ourselves, from the one God
> Who governs all.[31]

The *Didache,* the "Teaching of the Twelve Apostles," which
developed between the last third of the first century and probably
reached completion about A.D. 150, sketched a vision of unity and
mission in terms of: a common Faith, commonly held by all
(chapters 1-6); common worship and Sacraments (chapters 7-10);
common ministry and consecrated stewardship of Apostles and Prophets, bishops and deacons and laity (chapters 11-15); common hope
in the Lord (chapter 16); and—together with other apostolic pastors
and teachers[32]—the conduct of frequent Eucharistic assemblies in
common as well as consultative councils among them.[33]

> As this broken bread was scattered
>   upon the mountains,
> but was brought together
>   and became One,
> so let Thy Church be brought together
>   from the ends of the earth
>   into Thy Kingdom:
> for Thine is the glory and the power
>   through Jesus Christ, forever and ever.[34]

Dialogue: Sharing God's Gifts With Others

The mission of Christians, accordingly is to be and to perceive themselves as "the salt of the earth," who, like Christ, are to be luminaries *in* the world, *to* the world, and *for* the world in which they find themselves living.[35] The Lord, Saint Paul, and the early disciples were often in the Temple, the synagogues, and out among people of all walks of life and conditions.[36] They made a practice of praying, conversing, and dialoguing with sinners and the righteous, Jews and Gentiles alike. The primitive Church, as a whole, reached out constantly in living encounter.

One of the normal forms of that encounter was *apologia*—that is, formal defense and exposition of the Faith. The history and writings of Christian *apologia* are replete with examples of the luminary converts which such encounter gained for the Church from among the Hellenistic Jews, Hellenists, poets and philosophers, pagan priests and votaries, and the heterodox elite. Most notable among them were Aristeides, Tatian, Meliton, Athenagoras, and Justin. This last, known in the Church's annals as Saint Justin the Martyr, saw dialogue and encounter of various kinds as a singular duty following his conversion to Christianity. He reasoned that, by virtue of his God-given talents and the very manner of his conversion, he had the necessity above all to love his neighbor and, thus loving him, share with him the gift of faith with which God's holy grace had blessed him.[37] In order that "in every way . . . Christ is proclaimed," in the spirit of the Apostle to the Gentiles, Justin sought in the philosophies, religions, and heterodoxies of his era "whatever is true and righteous, whatever is honorable and pure and beautiful, whatever comes of good report, just so it be virtuous and praiseworthy" (Phil 1.18, 4.8).

Frequently, these encounters of *apologia* became formalized in the customary setting of the ancient schools. The Church of Alexandria created its own such academy, the great Catechetical School, "for the scientific treatment of Christian problems, open alike to Christians, catechumens, and seriously interested [but uncommitted] pagans."[38] In other words, the mainstream leadership of the Church sought out opportunities for potentially fruitful fields of Christian mission and growth. They took care neither to belittle nor to defame the heritages and cultures of those peoples among whom they ministered, and they differentiated carefully between the varieties of unbelievers. Many of these early pastors believed, like Justin, that the *spermatikos logos,* the seed of godly wisdom and right reason, is present in such societies, and even in their heterodox religions, from all time. The Church even canonized the best of them as "Christians before Christ"[39] and—just as Christ has brought to fruition and fulfillment the Law and Prophets of ancient Judaism—endeavored to correct, transform, and complete the essential good and validity which they found in the native teachings and practice.

Godly Discipleship in Unity

If they were zealous to discover the good in other teachings and cultures, the great pastors and teachers of the early Church were likewise careful to require that they, together with the faithful, "exceed the virtue of the Scribes and Pharisees." All was not "sweetness and light," for divisions and disputes arose out of a variety of causes: some by reason of typical interpersonal rivalries and ethnic jealousies, and others on account of more serious, religious differences. The standard for the followers of the Way was stricter precisely because of the overriding twin calls of the Lord for godly discipleship and unity and for their credibility of witness to the world. The concern was fundamental and the reproof for the wayward was severe indeed:

> As Children of the Light (cf. Eph 5.8) which is of truth, flee from divison and wrong teaching: where the shepherd is, follow (cf. Jn 10.10-12). . . . For as many as belong to God, to Jesus Christ, these are with the bishop. As many as repent and come to the unity of the Church, these also will belong to God, so that they may be living in accordance with Jesus Christ. Do not be deceived, my brethren: if anyone follows a maker of schism, that one "will not inherit the Kingdom of God" (1 Cor 6.9,10). . . .
>
> God does not dwell where there is division and wrath. I

exhort you to do nothing with a partisan spirit.[40]

Brethren, let us now, therefore, at last repent and take sober thought for what is good. . . . We must commend ourselves to outsiders in righteousness, lest the Name be blasphemed on account of us (cf. Is 52.5, Mt 18.7, Eph 6.6, Rom 2.24). . . .

In what is the Name blasphemed? In your failure to do what I desire!

For, when outsiders hear from our lips the oracles of God, they marvel at their beauty and greatness. But when they observe that our actions are unworthy of the Word we utter, they turn to blasphemy, saying the Faith is a myth and a deception. . . . When they see that we not only do not love those who hate us, but even do not love those who love us, they laugh us to scorn, and the Name is blasphemed.[41]

There is no greater scandal, the Fathers of the Church consistently believed and taught, than disunity among those who have joined in the Covenant and bear the Name of Christ. Certainly, they would find no common ground with one modern observer's suggestion that ecumenical mission, the age-old "movement toward oneness . . . is abnormal, and to recognize it as such would be an honest step forward."[42]

It was the Church leadership's overriding pastoral concern for godly discipleship and unity, within the Eucharistic fellowship of the Lord's ever-reconciling Body and Blood, which gave rise to the consultative councils and synods and to the canons and doctrinal confessions which were their fruit. Their intent was to develop both a basic understanding of the teachings of the Covenant and the pastoral legislation necessary for godly discipleship of clergy and laypersons alike, in conformance with Christ's Way, Truth and Life. In a letter to his brother-bishop, Domnos of Antioch, and to suffragan bishops in Libya, Saint Cyril of Alexandria gave his views of the value which the canons and conciliar professions held for the Church, as a Body and for the benefit of individual members:

Every one of our efforts in the Church can benefit from the rule of canonical discipline, for, instead of causing us embarrassment or disparagement, their witness [of the Church as a whole] will relieve us and gain us the commendation of fair-minded persons.

Who, after all, would not rather accept an impartial decision which, judged rightly and in keeping with the law [of Christ], merits praise and, for that very reason, is not reprehensible?[43]

This is not to belie the human frailty of the Church's institutions, even including the Lord's anointed, or to allege that all is "perfect within the visible structures of the Church."[44] The whole Tradition of the Church, including Scripture, affirms without dissent that only Christ the Lord is the Head and Guarantor of the Church. Even the decrees and canons "of a 'formally ecumenical' synod are accepted on the plane of the *oikonomia* of [church] discipline. . . . [They become] recognized and confirmed [when] received and lived by the People of God and integrated into the Eucharistic community by [the local bishop] . . . who 'presides in love.'. . ."[45]

Overall, the theology and canonical approaches of Orthodoxy, in continuity with the early Church, reflect an existential, down-to-earth pastoral recognition of the human condition and the mission of the Church:

The basic Orthodox attitude [is] reflected in the conception of sin, . . . [not] as a violation of the divinely established legal relationship between God and man. . .[but instead] as a diminution of essence, a loss of substance . . . of the original image (*eikona*) of God, that which man is and ought to be.

Redemption, therefore, is not primarily the restitution of a legal relationship. . . . Rather, it is the fulfillment, renewal, transfiguration. . . . of man's being. . . . Awareness of the overflowing fullness of divine love drives away all thought of any schemes of [legalistic] reckoning and satisfaction. . . .

Similarly, the Eastern Church has never thought of Judgment Day in the strictly juristic terms so customary in the West. . . . There is only confidence in grace and in the ''love of man—*philanthropia*,'' which is an attribute of the divine Logos . . . and, in addition, prayer for divine mercy.[46]

The Church's understanding of the Covenant is found in the conception of the relationship of the Son of God to the Father and to humankind. The Messiah, *ho Philanthropos,* is sent by the Father to restore—God-to-Man, and Man-to-man, so to speak—the wholeness of the divine image which, from the moment of creation, is implanted in each and in the whole of humanity. The Church constitutes that promise which God Himself can neither withdraw nor break, and as such can only be broken and distorted by the individual human person or community unilaterally, in the exercise of free will that God has given humankind. This free will may be either for the good or the ill of one's self and the rest of creation. The stewardship of the Church is to bring to fulfillment, among her faithful and the whole of the *oikoumene,* the steadfast ''covenant love'' of Yahweh as a new creation transfigured in holy fellowship and mutual giving and receiving of the Lord's gifts.

O Lord our God, save Thy people and bless Thy inheritance to them. Guard the fullness of Thy Church, and sanctify us who are consumed by the zeal for Thy House. Glorify them with Thy godly might, and do not desert us, for in Thee do we trust.[47]

NOTES

[1]Both directly and symbolically, the Ecumenical synods and the great Fathers of the undivided Church, East and West, have exercised the primary pastoral and teaching authority, especially for the Churches of the ancient Catholic tradition. As theologians who "pray theology" and view theology as above all the Word of God, the ancient Fathers have been seen traditionally as the successors to the prophets of the Old Testament who venerate, live, and "hold true the Covenant" which is found within the *consensus fidelium*, the right deposit of holy revelation among the people of God for all time. Cf. Jaroslav Pelikan, "Some Definitions," *The Christian Tradition, 2: The Spirit of Eastern Christendom (600-1700)* (Chicago, 1977), p. 3; and John Meyendorff, "Orthodox Theology Today," *Living Tradition* (Crestwood, N.Y., 1978), pp. 167-86.

[2]Saint Hilary of Poitiers, *ad Constantium Augustum*, 2.9; PL 10.

[3]The Communion Hymn for the Divine Liturgy, according to the traditional observance of the Eastern Orthodox Church on Epiphany Feastday.

[4]From the *Anaphora* Prayer of Living Remembrance, for the Invocation of the Holy Spirit upon the Eucharistic Gifts (*"Epiklesis"*), in the Divine Liturgy of the Eastern Orthodox Church.

[5]Ibid., in the solemn Offering of the Eucharistic Gifts.

[6]From the Liturgy of the Word prayer preceding the antiphonal, congregational proclamation of the Lord's Beatitudes, in the Divine Liturgy of the Eastern Orthodox Church.

[7]Lk 1.48-49,55,70-72,75-79.

[8]Most specifically, Mt 16.13,16-18, 18.18-22, 28.18-19; Jn 20.19-23; Acts 1.8; 2 Cor 13.10; Eph 3.7ff; Col 1.25ff; 2 Tim 1.6,11-14.

[9]From the *Anaphora* Prayer of Eucharistic Commemoration of the Living of "the holy, catholic, and apostolic Church," especially "every episcopacy of the Orthodox . . . [and] our God-loving Bishop . . ." in the Divine Liturgy of the Eastern Orthodox Church.

[10]From the Divine Liturgy Prayer of Humble Petition "with bowed head," following the congregational praying of the Lord's Prayer.

[11]Saint Irenaios of Lyons, *Against Heresies* 4.26.5; PG 7.

[12]Saint Vincent of Lerins, *Communitorium* 2.1; PL 50.

[13]Saint Basil the Great, *On the Holy Spirit* 27.66; PG 32. Also cf. 2 Pet 1.20-21.

[14]This process of the whole person's pilgrimage, in Christ, to advance "from glory to glory"(2 Cor 3.18) Saint Gregory called *epektasis* (ref. Phil 3.13), in his *Life of Moses*. This work was referenced in *From Glory to Glory: Texts from Gregory of Nyssa's Mystical Writings,* ed. Jean Danielou and Herbert Musurillo, S.J. (New York, 1961), pp. 56-71.

[15]From the Liturgy of the Word festal hymns accompanying the Entrance and Procession of the Holy Gospel, as observed in the Divine Liturgy of the Eastern Orthodox Church on Pentecost (Holy Trinity) Sunday, in celebration of the Church's birthday.

[16]From the Creed of Nicaea-Constantinople (A.D. 325/381).

[17]Paul Evdokimov, "Fundamental Desires of the Orthodox Church vis-a-vis the Catholic Church," trans. Ruth Dowd, R.S.C.J., *Concilium/14-Do We Know The Others (Ecumenical Theology)* (New York, 1966), pp. 70, 72.

[18]The *Creed.*

[19]From the Eucharistic Prayer of the Fraction of the Lamb, in preparing reception of Holy Communion during the Divine Liturgy of the Eastern Orthodox Church.

[20]Hamilcar Alivizatos, "Basic Orthodox Demands on the Roman Church," trans. Theodore L. Westow, in *Concilium/14* as above, p. 61.

[21]Evdokimov, "Fundamental Desires," p. 70.

[22]For greater detail and insight into the traditional Orthodox attitudes on this subject and one local Orthodox church's views on the application historically of *akribeia* and *oikonomia,* see Chapter Six: "Theological Presuppositions for Orthodox Ecumenism."

[23]Dean Barry Till, *The Churches Search for Unity* (Middlesex, England, 1972), p. 451.

[24]Ibid., pp. 450, 84-85. This flexibility of approach as to the issue of communion is not merely an antiquarian fact or concern. In the modern era, various Orthodox sees have withheld or accepted canonical relations with one another, while remaining in communion with other local churches which do not recognize their status. Recent, even continuing examples include: the relations within Orthodoxy in the wake of the partial schisms, during the last century, of the local churches of Greece and Bulgaria; the self-asserted autonomy and breaking of communion by the "Russian Orthodox Church Outside of Russia," which continues to this day; the self-asserted autonomy and partial isolation (1924-1970) of

the Russian-American "Metropolia," in reaction to the Soviet Communist regime's subjugation of the Church in the former Russian Empire; the variety of Eastern European and Ukrainian emigre church bodies which have broken ties with their former mother churches; and the Western-rite "Orthodox Catholic Church of France" which was established under the Romanian patriarchal jurisdiction, but remains unrecognized as in canonical status by other Orthodox churches.

Some of these church bodies are either independent for all practical purposes or under the canonical umbrella of one local church. They are viewed generally as being legitimate in their expression of the Orthodox tradition, but frequently lack certain canonical attributes and status. These are, however, to be distinguished from the variety of "autogenic Orthodox" religious bodies which have had no basic origin in or connection with the historic and canonical Orthodox churches, yet claim either Eastern or Roman Catholic antecedents and "Apostolic succession." Such groups are most frequently found in America, Western Europe, Africa, and Eurasia among assemblies of former Protestants and Roman Catholics, but remain unrecognized by all of the historic and canonical Churches of Eastern Orthodoxy and Roman Catholicism. Ref. Peter Anson, *Bishops at Large—Some Autocephalous Churches of the Past Hundred Years* (London, 1964); Henry R. T. Brandreth, *Episkopi Vagantes and the Anglican Church,* (London, 1947); and Archimandrite Seraphim, *The Quest for Orthodox Church Unity in America,* (New York, 1973).

[25]Cf. note no. 8 above.

[26]From the first prayer of the *Anaphora,* Eastern Orthodox Divine Liturgy. Cf. Jer 17.26, 33.11; Gal 6.16; Eph 2.14; Phil 4.7; Heb 13.15; 1 & 2 Tim 1.2; Tit 1.4.

[27]*Didache* 4.3.

[28]"Apostolic Canons" 65, 46: *Rudder,* pp. 1-154; *CJC,* pp. 230-33.

[29]*CJC,* 230.

[30]*Letter to Diognetos,* author unknown, c. A.D. 150, Chapter 5.1-10, 6.1, *ECF/B,* 54; *FEF/J,* Vol. One, 40-l; *CJC,* 232-33.

[31]Justin Martyr, *First Defense and Exposition of Christian Faith and Practice,* Chapter 14.3-4, *FEF/J,* 1, 52.

[32]Ancient Homily attributed as "Second Letter to the Corinthians" of Saint Clement of Rome, 17.3; Saint Ignatios of Antioch, Letter to Ephesians 13.1, To Polycarp 4.2; *Didache* 14.1, 16.2. *AF-G,* 1, pp. 139, 180; *AF-S,* pp. 69, 81, 117, 317-18.

[33]Ibid., above.

[34]*Didache* 9.4, *ECF/B*, p. 50.

[35]Mt 5.14-16; Phil 2.15; 1 Cor 9.22.

[36]Acts 2.46-47, 13.13-15, 21.26, 25.8. Cf. Mt 26.55/Mk 14.49/Lk 22.53/ Jn 18.20.

[37]*Dialogue with Tryphon the Jew,* Chapters 38 & 93, cited in *CJC,* pp. 235-36.

[38]*CJC,* p. 243.

[39]Saint Justin Martyr, *1st Defense,* Chapter 8; *ECF/B*, pp. 60, 64. The extent of this canonization can be seen in the fact that the philosopher Plato, among others of the pre-Christian era and religious traditions outside of the Covenant, is venerated within the Eastern Orthodox Church.

[40]Saint Ignatios, "Letter to the Philadelphians" 2, 3, 7.2, 8.1.2; *AF-S,* pp. 104-07.

[41]Saint Clement of Rome, 2 Corinthians 13.1-4, *ApFrs./Sp.,* p. 66.

[42]Ann Patrick Ware, S.L., "Response" to "Denominational Loyalities and Ecumenical Commitment: A Personal View," by Robert G. Stephanopoulos, *Journal of Ecumenical Studies* (1980).

[43]The *Rudder,* p. 915.

[44]As alleged, by Ware, above, to be the traditional Orthodox perspective of their Church's institutional life, "Response," p. 644.

[45]Evdokimov, "Fundamental Desires,"p. 70.

[46]Ernst Benz, "Dogma," *The Eastern Orthodox Church: Its Thought and Life,* trans. Richard & Clara Winston (Chicago, 1963), pp. 51, 52-3.

[47]The Liturgy of the Word "Prayer of the Second Antiphon," preceding the Hymn of the Incarnation ("O Only-Begotten Son and Word of God"), and the Celebrant's Invocation of the Lord's Blessing, after the community's reception of the Eucharist, in the Eastern Orthodox Divine Liturgy. Originating in the ancient Jewish liturgies, the prayer comprises verses from the Psalms: 27.9, 25.8/69.9, and 25.2/26.1.

CHAPTER FIVE:

Exemplars of the Ecumenical Tradition

Blessed are the peacemakers, for they shall be called the children of God. . . .

If you are bringing your gift offering to the Altar [of God], . . . first be reconciled with your brother. Only then come to offer your gift.

Be quick to make up your differences with those who are in opposition to you, while you are still together in the Way, lest you yourself be delivered over to the Judge. . . .

For if you love and greet only your brothers, those who love you, what merit is that to you? . . . What are you doing that even the Gentiles do not already do?

Of the one to whom much is given, much more is expected and required. Of the one to whom men commit much [in trust], much more will they demand.

You are to be perfect, even as your heavenly Father is perfect.[1]

Commenting on Saint Dionysios of Alexandria, one of the lesser-ranked Church Fathers, an authority has suggested that, on the contrary, he should be listed among the greatest of them. His most outstanding contribution, the commentator observed, was his example as pastor not only to his own flock, but also with the various pagan, heterodox, schismatic and heretical groups of his time. He exhibited to the world both the integrity and the moderation of the Way. "There reigns over his conduct that pure Spirit of the Gospel which proves that the virgin age of the Church was not yet of the past."[2]

As zealous as Saint Dionysios was in this ministry, his was by no means a unique attitude and pastoral witness. Despite occasional lapses, even some of those who appeared to be the most uncompromising of all showed in their pastoral works an ecumenical awareness of the difference between an honest concern, abiding in love, for unity and integrity of faith, on the one hand, and

95

that intolerant fanaticism which, on the other hand, is unwilling
to accept diversity or risk-taking. The early Fathers made allowance
for human frailty, being willing to set aside both strict logic and
canonical norms in the interest of reconciling to the Church those
who had strayed:

> Once a heretic, who had been baptized [by his sect of
> origin] in the Name of the Holy Trinity, has been taught in
> the Faith, let him be confirmed in the Church by profession
> and Chrismation only. . . . Others, however, coming from those
> who deny the Trinity or teach [of God] ambiguously, are to
> be baptized as anew. . . .
>
> And let the Catharist [heretical] clergy, once hands have
> been laid upon them, remain in their orders . . . when they
> will to adhere in faith to the doctrines of the catholic and
> apostolic Church.[3]

Even Saint Cyprian, stern hierarch of ancient Carthage and
a rigorist in opposition to admitting potential validity of efficacy
to sacramental rites performed among non-Orthodox communities,[4] did not hesitate to confess humbly that his was not the
infallible word:

> In regard to this matter, *each of us bishops should bring
> forward his opinion,* judging no one and depriving no one
> of the right of Communion if he should think differently. *For
> neither does any one of us set himself up as a bishop of the
> bishops,* . . . since every bishop has his own free will to the
> unrestrained exercise of his legitimate liberty and power [as
> a bishop].
>
> Rather, let us all await the judgment of our Lord Jesus
> Christ, the One and the only One Who has both the power
> of settling us in the governance of His Church and of judg-
> ing our conduct in that capacity.[5]

He and the majority of the Fathers perceived the Lord's admonition to the disciples to "be merciful" as the reason to exercise
pastoral *oikonomia* in the management of His household, the

Church, as well as in dealing with those outside her temporal bounds. To this end, they heeded the call to come together "in frequent assemblies," not only in the celebration of the Eucharist, but also in regional and ecumenical councils and synods. There they prayed and consulted as One, shared their insights and pastoral experience, and came to consensus as to the needs of the whole. Such "frequent assemblies" of consultation and decision making, in succession to that of the holy Apostles in the Council of Jerusalem, constituted a hallmark of the Churches of the East and of Africa, in particular.

Three prime examples of this ecumenical vision and conciliar spirit of Christian mission are treated in the following pages. They include, as mentioned above, Saint Dionysios of Alexandria (Egypt), A.D. 200-265, whose ancient see has historically exercised primacy in the Church of Africa and once was accorded—in the whole of the undivided Church—the distinction of being "judge of the *oikoumene.*" The second to be examined is Saint Basil of Cappadocia, in Asia Minor (Turkey), A.D. 330-379, who ranks as one of a trinity of "The Great Hierarchs" of the whole Church. Last is the Synod of Carthage, more well-known for the Christian Church's confrontation with the Donatist and Pelagian sects, which convened in A.D. 418 and only adjourned its business six years later. The two saintly pastors and the African synod stand out in their witness for the need of the Church to deal reasonably wherever unity may be restored.

Saint Dionysios: The Gentle "Judge of the Oikoumene"

As one observer wryly commented a century ago regarding the fierce Cardinal Henry Manning of England, some converts are "more papal than the Pope, more Roman than Romulus and Remus." They tend to view any dissent as heterodoxy or even heresy. Diversity put in practice becomes to them incipient schism, and ecumenical encounter and relations are perceived as pacts with error or even with Satan himself.

Nothing could be further, however, from the spirit and character of the convert Saint Dionysios than such a caricature. Apparently born of a wealthy pagan family, he was one of the most fruitful products of the great Christian apologists' outreach to the Hellenist philosophers and social elite. He did not come easily, though, to the new Faith: "it was only after candid examination of the [whole range of] the current philosophies that Dionysios was induced to become a Christian."[6] Once convinced, he took eagerly to the Church and her service. He was a student of the philosopher-theologian Origen, and eventually followed him as head of the famed Catechetical School of Alexandria. At age forty-seven, the presbyter Dionysios was elected to the episcopal throne, which he occupied as his people's dedicated archpastor until his death less than twenty years later.

His tenure was during eventful times. The occasional respites of relative peace were punctuated by the persecutions which the Roman Emperors Decius and Valerian visited upon the Christian communities. Internally, the Church's progress was marred by the divisive Novatian, Sabellian, and chiliastic troubles. Rather than withdrawing from the fray, the learned and inquisitive bishop set out deliberately to keep himself "abreast of all the controversies, . . . and perused with an impartial mind the works of the great heretics . . . and heterodox productions."[7] His purpose was to become so familiar with the inner workings and ideas of the heretics and the heterodox that he would be uniquely qualified to inititate dialogue and deal with them pastorally, leading them into the Church.

When a parish presbyter in his archdiocese rebuked the hierarch for his open spirit of inquiry and dialogue, on the grounds that his "mind would be contaminated" thereby, Saint Dionysios refrained from reacting with the typical angry reprimand of a superior to an upstart subordinate.[8] Instead, he accepted the point humbly as an advice worthy of consideration and a counsel of caution well taken. After a vigil spent in intense prayer and reflection over the question, the saintly bishop was, nevertheless, strengthened in his ecumenical mission "by a vision that was sent from God" and was convinced more than ever that his study and outreach to the leaders and followers of false ways or heterodoxies could become "the cause and occasion" for them to accept the Orthodox Faith.[9] He also took the time to examine the writings and lifestyle of the Epicureans, with the result that he composed a thoughtful volume of his observations and helped others in their spiritual pilgrimages from that persuasion to the Church.

On one occasion, he sought fraternal advice from the holy Pope Xystus II of Rome[10] on an especially difficult pastoral problem. A legalistic convert, by then a lay leader in Saint Dionysios' jurisdiction, discovered that his original Baptism many years previous had been defective, because of anti-Trinitarian heresy among the sectarians from whom he had come. The man tearfully begged Saint Dionysios to assign him to repeat the catechumenate and to undergo severe penances. The bishop's reaction, as the man's spiritual father, was to attempt to reassure him that a long life of service and sacramental life had immersed him well in the Body of the Church and that the Lord had surely "endowed with adoption and grace" whatever canonical defects had previously existed. During the Eucharistic Liturgy, Saint Dionysios called the man forward "to receive the blessed . . . Body and Blood of our Lord Jesus Christ" and so let the matter end at the Altar of God, "in good conscience."[11] Unfortunately, neither his bishop's reassurances nor the Sacraments were sufficient to satisfy the man; but it was not for lack of his spiritual father's pastoral concern and effort that the overly scrupulous one was lost to the Church.

Challenged on another occasion by serious dissension and heretical teachings, he summoned all the parties together in a council which included all the parish clergy and lay leaders. For three days the dialogue took place on the matters in contention, the participants prayed together, and the Scripture was exegeted and preached. The Saint's exemplary moderation won the day, and unity was restored to the Alexandrian Church in those parts.[12]

Hating always the sin and never the sinner, condemning error but not the human person whose ways were distorted by error and sin, Saint Dionysios went to his death bed bemoaning the opposite spirit which he saw leading the Church once again into division:

Whereas Christ, Who is the good Shepherd, goes in quest of one who wanders, lost among the mountains, and calls him back even when he flees from Him, and is at pains to take him up on His shoulders when He has found him, we, on the contrary, harshly spurn such a one even when he approaches us. . . .

Wherefore, let us not thrust from us those who seek; . . . but let us rather receive them gladly, . . . and make up again what is defective in them.[13]

Saint Basil: Zealot for the Lord's House

"Black-bearded, with bull-like head, heavy eyebrows, glittering eyes, small lips compressed tightly together, . . . possessed of a patrician" bearing[14] in his regal episcopal vestments—such is the stern, hierarchical image that characterizes Saint Basil the Great's traditional image. The ascetic founder of communitarian monastic life in the East, yet he was a nature lover and the author and compiler of some of the most tender and evocative prayers in the literature of worship. Tireless in his defiance of the rich, as the powerful defender and pastor of the poor and lowly, the robust image we traditionally associate with him belies the saint's actual condition as one who was forever plagued with sickness and was short-lived.

A man of paradox, he readily inspired love and hate alike. Saint Basil abominated heresy, schism, and any other "wolves in sheep's clothing" which might threaten to rend the seamless garment of his beloved Catholic and Orthodox Church of Christ. Still, he was as tireless an advocate of reconciliation efforts as Saint Paul the Apostle. Like Saint Dionysios, as a pastor he was willing—despite his zeal for the Church's canonical integrity and good order—to bend the rule and trust God to make up the difference, if certain basic needs of the Church's integrity were met. If twentieth century believers are unhappy over the divided state of Christianity and lack of movement in restoring catholic unity and orthodox Faith, they should be aware that—except for the modern phenomenon of denominationalism and frequent laissez-faire attitude towards Covenant and creedal integrity—this condition is nothing new to the Church. Saint Basil was just as upset over some of the same problems and felt, like his Alexandrian predecessor in the lists for ecumenical reconciliation, that undue rigorism and lack of fraternal love were to blame:

> There are things now which I hide in the bottom of my heart, in secret groaning over and bewailing the evil days in which we live, in that the greatest Churches—long united to one another in brotherly love—now, without any reason, are in mutual opposition . . .[15]
>
> We live in days when the overthrow of the churches seems imminent. . . . The Church does not edify [or] correct error, shows no sympathy for the weak, nor is a single defense offered of those brethren who are sound. No remedy is found either to heal this disease . . . or to act as a preventive against what we expect. Altogether the state of the Church (if I may use a plain figure, although it may seem too humble) is like an old coat: it is always being torn, but can never be restored to its original strength.[16]
>
> Apparently nothing is enough to stir us to anxiety for the welfare of one another. We jump on those who are fallen, we scratch and tear at wounds; we who are supposed to agree with one another launch the same curses [at one another] that are uttered by the heretics [at us]. Men who are in agreement on the most important matters are wholly severed from one another on some one, single point or other of little consequence. . . . [17]

Saint Basil urged that pastoral compassion be the "order of the day," so to speak, in the work of the Church and her leadership. He cited the precedents for pastoral *oikonomia* which the earliest Fathers, synods, and faithful of the Church had exercised in their concern for reconciliation of a wide variety of dissidents, heretics, and heterodox. These, he opined, represented a catholic consensus that was ample enough in witnessing the Covenant and in conciliatory results, so that his conscience was satisfied beyond a doubt.

At such a time [as we find ourselves in] there is need of great effort and diligence that the Churches may in some way be benefited. It is surely an advantage that parts hitherto severed should be united. And union would be effected the more if we were willing to accommodate our-selves to the weaker, where we can do so without injury to souls. . . .

We implore you, insofar as in you lies [the ability], to reduce the blasphemers to a small number, and to receive into communion all who do not assert the Holy Spirit to be created. . . . I really do not think that we ought to insist upon anything beyond [the Nicene Creed]. For I am convinced that by longer communication and mutual experience without strife, if anything more requires to be added by way of explanation, the Lord Who works all things together for good for them that love Him (Rom 8.28) will grant it.[18]

[It was] our very blessed Father, Athanasios, [who] distinctly declared that anyone expressing a wish to come over from the heresy of the Arians and accepting the Nicene Creed, is to be received without hesitation and difficulty, citing in support of his opinion the unanimous consent of the bishops of Macedonia and of Asia.

I consider myself bound to follow the high authority of such a man and those [others] who made the rule. With every desire on my own part to win the reward promised to peacemakers, I did enroll all who accepted that Creed in the lists of communicants. . . . [19]

Surely it will be quite sufficient . . . to confess the Faith put forward by our Fathers, once assembled at Nicaea, not omitting any one of its propositions, . . . not adding to that Creed, nor holding Communion with [outright heretics], to the end that the Church of God may be pure and without evil admixture of any tare. . . . [20]

After all, Saint Basil insisted, what are Christians all about, if not to care for and reconcile one to the other? How can a divided

Church witness to the one Covenant and to the Triune unity of the one God which is professed in the Nicene Creed? The Church's essential duty is unity and the making of peace, in prayer to the Lord:

> First, therefore, pray! And next, to the utmost of your ability, make exhortation . . . that reconciliation may be effected, . . . both to restore strength to the Church and to frustrate the rage of our foes.[21]
>
> The one great end of all who are really and truly serving the Lord ought to be to bring back to union the Churches now which "at sundry times and in diverse manners"(Heb 1.1) are divided from one another, . . . for nothing is so characteristically Christian as being the peacemaker, and for this reason the Lord has promised us peacemakers a very high reward. . . . [22]
>
> Take care not to cause union in one direction, and disunion in another, but rather try to restore the severed member to the original union. . . . [23]
>
> [For] the members of the Body of Christ have the same care for one another (1 Cor 12.25), according to the inborn spiritual communion of their sympathy. Wherefore, when one member suffers, all the members suffer with him. If one member is endowed with glory, all the members rejoice with him (1 Cor 12.26). For, after all, as parts in the whole are we individually in the Spirit of God, because we were all baptized in one Body and into the one Spirit.[24]

Moreover, the attitude and behavior of Christian pastors and faithful towards even the most obdurate of heretics, sectarians, and foes of the Church ought to be in strictest obedience always to the Lord's command to love our enemies. In terms of justice, the truth will win out, while we patiently maintain all possible ties:

> Nor do I think it absolutely our duty to cut off ourselves from those who do not receive the Faith, but rather to have

care for them in accordance with the old law of love, and in common consent [we must] address them and propose to them the Faith of the holy Fathers, and invite them to union.

If we succeed, we should be united in communion with them. . . . But if not, then, we may know at least who are the real authors of the conflict.[25]

Like Saint Dionysios, Saint Basil did not reserve these efforts for himself or feel that they were the concern and province only of the Church hierarchy. If it was to be successful, the movement to reunite the severed branches of the Vine had to be shared by all who were in the Church's ministry. Coming to the end of his stormy life and episcopal service, he took the time to commend the tireless efforts which a beloved parish presbyter had initiated in ecumenical outreach and reconciliation. Apparently, he was heartened by the prospect that his own concern for the integrity of the Lord's House would be continued through such efforts and zeal:

And you, blessed presbyter Euagrios, may you have the reward of the peacemaker, since you have long had so blessed an office as the object of your worthy desires and earnest efforts. . . . I will yield to none in my earnest wish and prayer to see the day when those who are one in sentiment shall all complete the same Assembly. In fact, it is monstrous [for anyone, as some do] to take pleasure in the schisms and divisions of the Churches, not at all considering the fact that the greatest of goods consists in the knitting together of the members of Christ's Body. But, alas! my own inability [to bring this to accomplishment] is just as real as is my desire to do so.

No one knows better than you do that time alone is the healer of those ills that time has brought to the present maturity, and a strong and vigorous treatment is necessary if we are to get at the root of the problem.[26]

Carthage: Synod of Ecumenical Charter

The fifth century assembly of the North African Churches, the Synod of Carthage, is unique in the annals of Church history in its specific contributions to the ecumenical movement. First of all, acting in a spirit akin to that of Saints Dionysios and Basil, the Synod offers direct and particular guidelines for official, church-wide efforts to restore Christian unity "among the Churches now divided." These canons and decrees represent probably the single greatest mandate and precedent, historically and canonically, for the essential thrust and *oikonomia* of the twentieth-century ecumenical movement. Secondly, although originally regional in scope (the Church of Africa), the Synod of Carthage acquires authority for all the Churches of the Orthodox Catholic Tradition by virtue of the official incorporation and endorsement of its basic canons and decrees by the Fourth, Sixth, and Seventh Ecumenical Synods (Chalcedon, A.D. 451, Constantinople, A.D. 680-81, and 2 Nicaea, A.D. 787).

The brief survey which follows does not attempt to cover the whole of the material concerned with the Synod's ecumenical efforts. The five main areas of ecumenical approaches are highlighted, together with pertinent excerpts and commentary.

As to the justification for ecumenical activity and the approach to be used, Canons **75/66, 76/67,** and **77/68**[27] proclaim that the Synod and, therefore, the Church must act pastorally in the furtherance of ecclesial unity:

When all things had been considered which seem conducive to the advantage of the Church, the Spirit of God suggesting and admonishing us, we determined to act leniently and peaceably with [the heretics and schismatics], although they were cut off from the unity of the Lord's Body by an unruly dissent, so that "perchance," as the Apostle says, when we have gathered them together with gentleness, "God should grant them the *metanoia* for the acknowledging of the truth" (2 Tim 2.25-26).

We decree that letters be dispatched on the part of our

Council, moreover, to the leaders of Africa . . . to ask them
to help their common mother, the Catholic Church, . . . and,
with Christian Faith, to investigate the facts in all regions . . .
and make all the facts concerning these matters known to
all who need such knowledge [in their ministry]. . . . In every
way, the catholic unity must be advanced and consummated
to the manifest profit of brotherly souls in those regions in
which they are living, . . . as the right to be saved has been
denied to no person.[28]

This initial proclamation is comparable in approach and scope
to the initiatives in our own times by the Ecumenical Patriarchate and her sister Churches (the great Patriarchal and Synodical Encyclicals of 1902, 1904, 1920, and 1973,[29] and by the Vatican II Council (1963-65) of the Roman Patriarchate and her depen-
dent churches (*Lumen Gentium* and *Unitatis Redintegratio*
Decrees).[30]

The next major ecumenical act (Canon **78**/69, Minutes-Act 5)
was to mandate official encounters with the heretical and schismatic
sects, specifically the "Donatists" and "Maximianists." This required that "delegations be sent on our part to their bishops, if
they have any, or to their laity, to proclaim peace and unity, without
which the salvation of Christians cannot be accomplished. Through
these legates all persons who have no reasonable ground to be in
opposition to the Catholic Church may, indeed, be made aware
of the evidence afforded . . . wherein they are quarreling with us,
the Catholic Church. . . . "[31] Likewise, the formula for these
dialogues and other approaches is on the basis of Christian peace
and equity, in the spirit of a common conciliar search for the truth.
The Orthodox delegation, the Synod Fathers decreed, is to advise
the dissident churchmen of these premises and convey the Church's
goodwill:

We have received authority from the Synod to talk with
you with a yearning to feel glad of your correction, since we
know that the Lord felicitates peacemakers (Mt 5.9) and
through the Prophet Isaiah (66.5) tells us to say to those who

hate and despise us these words: "You are our brethren."
So you ought not to scorn this peaceful suggestion which we
are making to you out of love.

If, on the other hand, you deem that your views are the
true ones, select for yourselves the representatives you want,
and we will select for ourselves those we want. And thus *let
a synod of both parties be held in a definite place and time,
and let that which separates us be examined peacefully, in
order that by the peaceful examination of the matter, an end
may be put to the error [of disunity], with the help of God,
after the truth has been made manifest.*

It is valuable to note that not only does the Synod not disallow
the ability of the canonical Church to enter into equitable dialogues,
in the context of a mutual and official council, with parties which
are outside the Church's communion, but, to the contrary, the
bishops of the Church are specifically directed to do so, if it is
felt that such action will serve to bring about ultimate unity.
Moreover, Canon **99**/91 also requires that each bishop and his
diocese should incorporate such an ecumenical program within
their own activities. "Each bishop [is to] meet with the leaders
of the Donatists in his own city, and/or associate [his ecumenical
efforts] with a neighboring bishop, that together they may meet
with them."[32]
On the matters of how to treat with and, eventually, to receive
back into communion the dissidents' hierarchy and clergy, the
Council disallowed the more rigorist approach which Pope Saint
Anastasios I of Rome and the churches of Italy had adopted in
the "Transmarine Council." Five specific canons (**77**/68, **110**/99,
128/117, **129**/118, and **130**/119)[33] allow liberal pastoral economy
in seeking out and bringing about the hoped-for reunion:

Whatever ones are clergy, providing their resolution is cor-
rected and [they are in truth] willing to come over to catholic
unity, in accordance with the voluntary choice and resolution of each individual catholic bishop [and] where this

appears to be conducive to the peace of Christians, re-admit
them in their own orders, just as also in previous times it
was evidently done . . . [that they may] be welcomed by
whatever means the catholic unity can be furthered.

Futhermore, provision was made for situations where, in the
event of reunion, conflicting jurisdictions might ensue between
the reuniting and the standing hierarchies and clergy, respectively.
Also, two key rights were basically recognized for those coming
into communion with the canonical Church, if, that is, the dissident church body's order was previously constituted. First, once
the bishop of a formerly schismatic or heretical community makes
the Orthodox confession of Faith and enters into communion on
terms of good faith with the canonical Church, he is entitled to
retain the territory of his jurisdiction as a canonical diocese. Second, the laity of that community are entitled to regular diocesan
and parish status with all their canonical rights as distinct, not
subject, communities of their own character and traditions. If not
heretofore constituted as distinct parish or diocesan communities,
then they are to come within the jurisdiction of the neighboring
diocese.[34]

Withal, the other side of *oikonomia* is the necessary application of *akribeia*, the exercise of the strict rule and correc-
tive action, where more moderate approaches fail or are not
applicable thereto. The Synod provided for *akribeia* in regard
to both her own and those outside the Church's communion.
On the one hand, according to Canons **131**/121, **132**/122,
133/123,[35] if bishops make no ecumenical effort at all and
"neglect [the courses of action necessary] to bring the places
belonging to their see into catholic unity," they are to be admonished by their brethren, the neighboring bishops. "If within six
months," however, the negligent bishops have still done nothing of substance towards resolving the problem, "then let that
territory [needing to be joined to catholic unity] belong to that
bishop who can win over the dissidents." Finally, if the negligent
bishop continues to procrastinate or fail to initiate appropriate
ecumenical efforts within his responsibility as a steward of the

Lord's unity, then no other canonical bishop "shall remain in communion with him until he does his duty."

On the other hand, Synod Minutes-Act 5 and the whole force of the canons provide that if peaceable, equitable, and patient efforts by the synods and bishops of the canonical Church are rejected, the heretical and schismatic parties are to be treated "firmly and deprivedly," and it will become "manifest to all that [they] are the faithless ones." Further ecumenical contact is to cease, unless and until the sectarians show repentance and a genuine desire to move towards unity in true faith.

Given the temper of the times and the general history of humanity's inhumanity towards any kind of dissidents, especially religious,[36] it is surprising to many observers to discover that a key concern enunciated by the Synod Fathers was for religious freedom of conscience. Unless dissidents or other nonbelievers aggravated and impinged upon the rights of the members and communities of the Church, her leadership shows a distinct aversion towards infringing upon the dictates of individual conscience. Like the later Canon 8 of the Seventh Ecumenical Synod (2 Nicaea), when the Church's pastors and teachers forbade the forcible conversion or other coercion of the Jews,[37] the Synod of Carthage (Canon 119) stresses that "the exercise of Christianhood" is to be undertaken "only by free choice." The canonist-commentator explains these decrees by reference to the Lord's own pastoral example and tolerance of others. The acceptance of Christianity is properly a "voluntary" act, it is observed, "for things that are done by constraint and under compulsion are not certain and permanent, but temporary and short-lived."[38] Without doubt, these are among the earliest and most authoritative proclamations of the right to religious liberty and freedom of conscience in the history of the Western world, and they would come into conflict with the normal proclivities of civil and ecclesiastical authorities alike for centuries yet to come.

Yet another example of pastoral compassion for those unable to fend for themselves is Canon 83 of the Synod. In the spirit of the Gospel and the *consensus patrum,* the Synod Fathers inveighed mightily against social injustices and admonished the emperor and all civil authorities to take specific political and social action to right wrongs then being perpetrated against the poor and lowly.[39] The bishops likewise reminded one another and the whole of the Church of the responsibilities which a Christian leadership has in this regard:

> To all of us it seemed advisable to petition the emperor to relieve the harsh treatment of the indigent at whose hardships the Church is ceaselessly annoyed. Let advocates be chosen with the provident attention of the bishops, empowered to protect [the poor and lowly] against the ungodly tyranny of the rich.

In summary, the essence of the Covenant—not the least of which are the above-mentioned exemplars of the Church's historic ecumenical and evangelical Tradition—witnesses eloquently and prophetically to the inherent need and justification for the movement in our own times to bring about unity, peace, freedom, and justice among the People of God. The fact that these voices speak across so many centuries does not diminish their relevance to the needs of this fractured religious and social world in which we live today. To the contrary, their witness can lend even greater urgency to our tasks and, given all the technological advantages and the greater potential for accurate communication which we enjoy, it should shame the Church and the Churches to heal the breaches which continue to exist after all these centuries.

> Remember, O Lord, those who work for the welfare of Thy holy Churches, and those who care for the poor, and send down Thy mercies upon us all. And grant that, with one mouth and one heart, we may glorify and praise Thy glorious and mighty Name: Father, Son, and Holy Spirit, one God, now and ever, unto all ages.
>
> Amen.[40]

NOTES

[1] Mt 5.7,9; 5.23-25, 43-47; Lk 12.48; Mt 5.48.

[2] A. Cleveland Coxe, D.D., *Ante-Nicene Fathers,* Vol 6, pp. 77-78.

[3] The Synods of Arles (A.D. 314)—Canon 8, 1 Nicaea (325 A.D.)—Canon 8, Laodicea (364 A.D.)—Canons 7 & 8. This zealous search to compromise justly, in Spirit and truth, in order "to find the middle way (μεσότητα τινα). . .to reach that sacred union (τό Θεῖον ἔργον τῆς ἑνώσεως)," was the same patient spirit of attempted reconciliation which Patriarch Photios I of Constantinople and Mark Eugenikos of Ephesos exhibited in their ninth and fifteenth century efforts, respectively, to accomplish the reunion of the ancient churches of East and West. Yet, ironically, both have been traditionally misrepresented as hardline foes of Eastern Orthodox-Roman Catholic unity. See: John Meijer, C.Ss.R., *A Successful Council of Reunion* (Thessalonike, 1975); Astergios Gerostergios, *Saint Photios the Great,* (Belmont, Ma., 1980); Constantine N. Tsirpanlis, *Mark Eugenicus and the Council of Florence: A Historical Re-evaluation of His Personality,* (New York, 1979), especially pp. 48-49.

[4] Along with many of his brethren of that era, Saint Cyprian judged the exercise of sacramental rites by heretical or schismatic clergy and their communities to be "unlawful and profane . . . inefficacious." The question provoked widespread disagreement. Another, positive view which was maintained by other Church Fathers is typified by the statement of Saint Optatus of Numidia (Libya):

> The workers can be changed, but not the [essence of the] Sacraments. If you, then, can see that all who are baptizing are workers, not Lords, and that the Sacraments are holy of themselves (*sacramenta per se esse sancta, non per homines*), rather than by reason of man's doing, what is it that you claim so urgently for yourselves . . . that you insist God excludes from his gifts? Admit that it is God who controls what is his own! ("Against the Donatist Schism" 5.4, A.D. 367; PL 11.883-1103).

[5] Proem by the Council President, "Acts of the Council of Carthage, Cyprian Presiding," A.D. 256, ref. *FEF/J,* pp. 240-41.

[6] S. D. F. Salmond, *Ante-Nicene Fathers* 6, p. 79.

[7] Ibid.

[8] The question of the position of the parish presbyter—and of the presbyters as a body—was, Saint Dionysios agreed, indeed a crucial one.

Clergy who surrender their spiritual individuality and local pastoral rights and responsibilities paralyze the Church's life by quenching the Spirit and neglecting the priesthood in Christ which they share. The admonition of Saint Jerome was: "It is a very bad custom in some churches for presbyters to be silent and to refrain from speaking in the presence of bishops, on the grounds that these latter would either be jealous of them or think it unbecoming to be listeners [to subordinates]. ' . . . let the *primus* hold his peace: you may all prophesy, one by one, that all may learn and all may be comforted; and the spirits of the prophets are subject to the prophets'" (Ep. 52).

In the ancient document *Apostolic Constitutions* (2, 28), the presbyters are called "the counsellors of the bishop and the crown of the Church . . . the council and senate of the Church." In Canon 22 of the Fourth Synod of Carthage the bishop was forbidden to ordain anyone without the advice of his clergy so that he might know the sense of the people of his parishes. The bishop was, first and foremost, president of the presbyteral council and archpastor of the body of the faithful, clergy and lay.

The customary relationship of the bishops to the presbyters of his diocese is summed up in *Antiquities of the Christian Church* (2, 19, 7): "Though the bishop was prince and head of the ecclesiastical senate and nothing could regularly be done without him, yet neither did he ordinarily do any public act relating to government and discipline of the Church, without their advice and assistance."

[9]*Ibid.*, p.79. Also, in the same volume, "The Works of Dionysios," Epistle 7—to Philemon, Presbyter, pp. 102-03.

[10]By the custom of the time, the bishops of three patriarchal sees—Alexandria, Carthage, and Rome—regularly used the title "Pope" (from Greek *papas*), signifying "father of a great, ancient metropolitan church." Today, only Alexandria and Rome retain the usage, although every Greek Orthodox priest is also known by the original *papas,* as spiritual father of his parish community.

[11]"The Works of Dionysios," Epistle 7, p. 103.

[12]Salmond, ibid., p. 79.

[13]"The Works of Dionysios: 'On the Reception of the Lapsed'," p. 120.

[14]Robert Payne, *The Holy Fire: The Fathers of the Eastern Church* (London, 1961), p. 137ff.

[15]"To the Neocaesareans," *The Nicene and Post-Nicene Fathers,* Vol 8 —Saint Basil: Letters and Select Works, trans. Bloomfield Jackson, (Grand Rapids, 1968), p. 245.

[16] "To the Presbyters at Tarsus," pp. 189-90.

[17] "To Bishop Epiphanios of Salamis," pp. 294-95.

[18] "To Presbyters at Tarsus," pp. 189-90

[19] "To the Neocaesareans," p. 245.

[20] "To Kyriakos, at Tarsus,"p. 190.

[21] "To Bishop Epiphanios," pp. 294-95.

[22] "To Kyriakos," p. 190.

[23] "To Bishop Epiphanios"pp. 194-95.

[24] "On the Holy Spirit," 26, p. 39.

[25] "To Bishop Eusebios of Samosata," pp. 196-97.

[26] "To the Presbyter Evagrios of Antioch," pp. 210-11.

[27] By way of explanation, the number in **bold print** refers to the numbering used in the *Rudder* text, while the second, light number refers to the numbering in the volume *7 Ecumenical Councils.*

[28] *Rudder,* pp. 648-49; *7 Ecumenical Councils,* pp. 475-76.

[29] See: Chapter 7 of this work, as well as *The Orthodox Church in the Ecumenical Movement: Documents and Statements 1902-1975,* ed. Constantin G. Patelos (Geneva, 1978), pp. 27-43ff., 59-65, and *Istoria tes Oikoumenikes Kineseos,* Basil Th. Stavridis (Athens, 1964), pp. 116-27.

[30] *The Documents of Vatican II, 1963-65,* eds. Walter M. Abbott, S.J. and Joseph Gallagher (New York, 1966), pp. l5, 30-37, 78-79, 84, 336-66.

[31] The *Rudder,* pp. 650-51; *7 Ecumenical Councils,* p. 445.

[32] The *Rudder,* pp. 661-62; *7 Ecumenical Councils* pp. 487-88.

[33] The *Rudder,* pp. 649-50 & 698-99, 668-69 & 697-700; *7 Ecumenical Councils,* pp. 476-77 & 499, 492-93 & 499-500.
There is also evidence to indicate that an even more liberal exercise of *oikonomia* was used in certain areas. Some of the sects which chose to (re)unite with the canonical Church had lost or not maintained the regular exercise of apostolic succession in Holy Orders. As prescribed by Canons 18 and 19 of the Synod of Sardica (present-day Sofia, Bulgaria), which assembled in 344 A.D., Presbyters and other clergy who had been "ordained" by assemblies of presbyters or by non-apostolic hierarchs of one kind or another were accepted, *kat'oikonomian,* in their orders as is and, following profession of Orthodox faith and laying on of hands by a canonical bishop, were allowed to administer the Sacraments and to pastor regular communities.

[34] Ibid.

[35] The *Rudder,* pp. 700-02; *7 Ecumenical Councils,* pp. 50l-02.

[36]See *CJC,* 41-47, 101-08, 251-52; Stanton A. Coblentz, *The Long Road to Humanity,* (New York, 1959); and H. W. Haussig, *A History of Byzantine Civilization,* trans. J. M. Hussey (New York, 1971), pp. 45-49.

[37]The *Rudder,* pp. 438-39; *7 Ecumenical Councils,* p. 561.

[38]The *Rudder,* p. 673; *7 Ecumenical Councils,* p. 496.

[39]The *Rudder,* p. 653; *7 Ecumenical Councils,* p. 479.

[40]The final *Anaphora* "Prayers of Intercession for the Living," preceding the congregational praying of the "Lord's Prayer," in the Divine Liturgy of the Eastern Orthodox Church.

Theological Presuppositions for Orthodox Ecumenism

Introduction[1]

The Church of Christ is the holy and infallible Body within which, and through which, the work of man's salvation is realized.

The whole institution of the Church is held together and constituted by the indwelling Holy Spirit, Who heals what is weak and makes up that which is wanting. The Church, as the ark of grace and truth, expressing herself through the proper channels and dispensing the treasure of divine grace, leads the faithful to salvation.

For this work the Church uses not only *akribeia* (strict application of canon law), but also *oikonomia* (economy, modified and flexible application of canon law), since "there are two kinds of government and correction in the Church of Christ: the one is called *akribeia*, the other *oikonomia* and condescension; with these the stewards (*oikonomoi*) of the Spirit guide souls to salvation now with the one, now with the other."[2] Likewise, according to Patriarch Dositheos of Jerusalem, "Church affairs are viewed in two ways, by *akribeia* and by *oikonomia*, so that when they cannot be settled by *akribeia*, they are settled by *oikonomia*."[3]

Meaning of Akribeia and Oikonomia

The terms *akribeia* and *oikonomia* are customarily employed in theological terminology to denote two different attitudes taken by the Church in making use of the means of salvation:

The first of the two terms, *akribeia*, denotes the Church's strict adherence to the canonical ordinances concerning each believer.[4]

The other term, *oikonomia*, denotes the Church's loving care towards her members who transgress her canonical ordinances,[5] and also towards those Christians who are outside her Body and wish to enter it.[6]

Akribeia

The whole situation and life of man in relation to God is regulated ecclesiastically according to Gospel teaching and the Church's canons. This means that in the meeting between man and God who acts, the relationship is a relationship of canonicity and *akribeia*. This requires on the one hand the correct and full acceptance of revealed truth and grace, and on the other, the correct and full conformity in freedom to the canons laid down by the Church.

Oikonomia

Apart from the meaning which concerns us here, the term *oikonomia* also denotes the divine purpose or *prothesis* (Eph 1.10, 3.9-11),[7] the mode of existence of the one Godhead in Trinity through mutual indwelling *(perichoresis)*,[8] its broad action in the world through the Church,[9] divine Providence,[10] the Savior's Incarnation,[11] the whole redeeming work of our Lord Jesus Christ[12] and all the operations through which human nature was made manifest in the Son,[13] from the time of His Incarnation to His Ascension into heaven.[14]

In particular, the Church Fathers and other ancient ecclesiastical writers use the term *oikonomia* primarily to designate the Incarnation of our Lord as a truth of faith, contained in certain doctrinal formulations of the Ecumenical Synod and in other contemporary declarations of faith.[15] The Seventh Ecumenical Synod uses a particular dogmatic formula to ascribe how faith penetrates into the "saving economy" of our Lord Jesus Christ.[16] Economy as an object of faith is also mentioned in other texts of the Seventh Ecumenical Synod,[17] along with the whole redeeming work of Christ.[18]

In the same way, since the Church continues to make available to the faithful the redeeming work of our Lord Jesus Christ in the world, the holy Fathers and ecclesiastical writers also give the name "economy" to the work of the Church and describe it as "saving economy," "ecclesiastical economy," "economy of the Church."[19]

It is, therefore, the Church's right and mandate, copying the economy of Christ and displaying, as a mother according to grace, an especial loving-kindness, to employ economy when dealing with the diverse weaknesses and shortcomings of men in their faith and the Christian life.

Economy can be regarded either as a kind of deviation from the full and exact acceptance of the saving truth—a deviation permitted to a man because of his inability to grasp this truth completely and apply it in his life; or else as a deviation from the exact and full observance of canon law. Yet at the same time economy does not abolish exactness, since the Church through her love and her sanctifying divine grace makes up all that is lacking in the life of her members.

However, things being what they are, and it being utterly impossible to broaden the content of revelation, economy cannot be more demanding than exactness *(akribeia)*. . . .

Economy in the Sacraments: Within the Church and Outside of the Church

Thus *akribeia* and *oikonomia* are the two poles determining the limits within which the Church's work unfolds, in regard both to her own members and to the Christians outside her ranks. They constitute the two main ways in which the Church can advance in the use of the means of salvation.

The problems concerning exactness and economy have attained vast proportions in contemporary church life; for never before in the Church's history have the issues of interchurch and interconfessional relations, of the *rapprochement* and union of Christians, and of ecumenical unity, been raised so persistently and in so many different guises.

The economy employed by our holy Orthodox Church has its roots in Holy Scripture and Tradition; it has been defined and fixed by decisions of local and ecumenical synods and developed by the Fathers of the Church, and also by subsequent and contemporary Orthodox theologians, and has been carried into practice by the autocephalous Churches.

This practice has two sides to it: dogmatic and canonical. As we have said, the origin and basis of ecclesiastical economy is the Incarnation of our Lord Jesus Christ and His entire work of redemption, which started at the Incarnation as an act of divine condescension and philanthropy.[20] Ecclesiastical economy takes its origin from the spirit of God's love and mercy towards men and is so governed by the same spirit, in the words of our Savior: "For God so loved the world, that He gave His only-begotten Son, that whosoever believes in Him might not die, but have everlasting life" (John 3.16) and "I desire mercy, and not sacrifice" (Mt 9.13).

The Fathers of the Church use the term *oikonomia* above all in the sense of God's condescending to man in the Incarnation.[21] We find this sense in Saint Athanasios,[22] Saint Basil,[23] Saint Cyril of Alexandria,[24] Theodotos of Ankyra,[25] Saint Maximos the Confessor,[26] Saint John of Damascus,[27] and Saint Photios.[28] Many other Fathers call the Son's Incarnation "the mystery (or Sacrament) of the economy," or "the great mystery of the economy"—to quote the exact doctrinal terms used by the Quinisext Ecumenical Synod.[29]

The divine Apostles, bearing in mind that, through the Incarnation and sacrifice of Christ the Savior, God wants "all men to be saved and to come to the knowledge of truth" (1 Tim 2.4), acted through the gift of sanctifying divine grace and through various means of salvation to save straying sinners, either by the canon of *akribeia* or by the canon of *oikonomia*.

Following the example of the Apostles "as good stewards of the manifold grace of God" (1 Pet 4.10), the leaders of the holy Churches during the first centuries undertook in the same way to solve the problems relating to the saving work of the Church. It is clear from the canonical and patristic works that the main purpose pursued in the practice of economy was to prevent the door of salvation from being shut to anyone (1 Tim 2.4, Acts 14.27), and to ensure on the contrary that the gates of heaven were opened wide to every believer, thereby rendering easier the return into the bosom of the Church of all who had strayed.[30]

Many are the synodical and patristic canons which make use

of the term *oikonomia*, or similar terms, to describe the Church's condescension. This condescension is displayed not only towards the living but the dead as well, with a view to reinstating them after their death.

That the Church was primarily concerned with saving souls in its legislation on economy and its practice of the same is shown not only by the canons and their application but also by the way in which a whole succession of Fathers and ecclesiastical writers understood, interpreted, and applied the principle of economy. In addition to the decisions already mentioned, reference should be made also to the canonical ordinances of Saint Gregory of Nyssa,[31] as well as to guidelines and interpretations given by Saint John Chrysostom,[32] Saint Cyril of Alexandria,[33] Theodotos of Ankyra,[34] Saint John the Faster (Jejunator),[35] Eulogios of Alexandria,[36] Saint Maximos the Confessor,[37] Saint Anastasios of Sinai,[38] Saint Nikephoros the Confessor,[39] Saint Theodore of Studios,[40] Saint Photios,[41] Nicholas Mystikos,[42] and finally the great commentaries on the holy canons and notably those of Zonaras,[43] Balsamon[44] and Aristenos[45] . . .

Nicholas Mystikos . . . writes: "Economy is salvatory condescension, . . . stretching out a helping hand to raise the fallen . . . an imitation of divine philanthropy.[46] . . . Zonaras, Balsamon and Aristenos stress this saving aim, . . . "to bring back the lost sheep" to the fold of the Church.[47]

Economy in the Reception of Heretics and Schismatics

It can be seen from the above that there are two distinct levels on which economy is practiced. The first consists of the ordinary means applied, with logic and prudence, by the Orthodox Church for the strengthening and guidance of her faithful flock along the path of salvation; while the second consists of the provision of sanctifying grace by the Church in special circumstances both to her own faithful and to those Christians outside her Body who desire to enter within.

In this second case, economy reveals the Church as the ark and steward *(oikonomos)* of divine grace, dispensing it **in** exceptional circumstances to those who have received the Sacraments either within the Church or outside it, but without fulfilling the conditions laid down by the Church for their salvation.

Economy, as an exceptional means of salvation, goes beyond the rigid canonical bounds of *akribeia* in the sacramental life of the Church. It may thus be said that economy constitutes an exceptional type of action, yet of the same nature as the action invoked in bestowing the Sacraments; it reinforces the effect of each one of the Sacraments by completing or confirming them under certain circumstances, notably when they have been imperfectly performed. In this manner, economy may be considered as completing what is lacking and, through divine grace, perfecting that which has not been performed according to *akribeia*.

In ecclesiastical legislation both old and new, as in the writings of the theologians, the term *oikonomia* is used in this special sense of the dispensation by the Church of sanctifying grace exceptionally, in certain cases. The term *oikonomia* is likewise used in various senses, also expressed by the words *synkatabasis* (condescension), *pronomion* (privilege), *eleemosyne* (charitable giving), *philanthropia* (philanthropy, loving-kindness), *apolysis* (loosing), *syngnome* (pardon, forgiveness), *lysis* (freeing), *aphesis* (remission), etc.

But all of these terms have their own particular meaning, which does not cover the bestowing of sanctifying grace. They are limited to matters of a disciplinary or administrative nature and, in general, to matters pertaining to canonical relations and the moral behavior of the faithful.

The Orthodox Church has applied *akribeia* and *oikonomia* in dealing both with her own members and with the non-Orthodox (heterodox). In the case of the latter, she has always clearly distinguished between the different types of heterodox whom she has received into her bosom—some of them returning in penitence to their Father's House, like the Prodigal Son (Luke 6.11-32), while she has forgiven others in the Name of Christ, even those who have caused her much sorrow (2 Cor 2.5-11). For she has not considered them to be in permanent schism and separation from her, but only temporarily, "for Satan must not be allowed to get the better of us" (2 Cor 2.11, NEB).

"That all may be one"

The Church being one, all who are alienated from her may be considered as standing on different rungs of one and the same ladder leading up to her when they desire to return to the Church. More precisely, we could say that the Holy Spirit acts upon other Christians in very many ways, depending on their degree of faith and hope.

It is, consequently, clear that Christians outside the Orthodox Church, even when they do not maintain their faith intact and immaculate, nonetheless keep their link with Christ, through their unwavering hope in him. These Christians rejoice "with the joy of hope" (Rom 12.12). They confess that, through hope, they possess Christ, the common Lord, along with all Christians, because the confession of Christ unites us all, He being our common Lord and the hope of our final salvation.

To understand more clearly the relationship between the faithful outside and within the Church, we must turn to the way in which Scripture describes the joy of those who find themselves in the House and in the courts of the Lord. Within the Lord's House, light and warmth exist in abundance and strength, so that great joy is felt by those who approach.

This light shines afar, even into the outer darkness: "The very word of him who hears the words of God, who with staring eyes sees in a trance the vision from the Almighty. How goodly are your tents, O Jacob, your dwelling-places, Israel, like long rows of palms, like gardens by a river, like lign-aloes planted by the Lord, like cedars beside the water!" (Num 24.4-6, NEB). The Psalmist distinguishes between the House of the Lord and His courts, saying: "How dear is Thy dwelling-place, Thou the Lord of hosts! I pine, I faint with longing for the courts of the Lord's Temple" (Ps 83.1-2, 84.1-2, NEB).

The light and the joy of the Lord's House and His courts extend a long way off, inasmuch as their radiance is not abruptly blocked, nor does the outer darkness begin suddenly and all at once. In other words, the darkness of the lack of grace seeps

gradually over those who are outside the Church. Grace is not completely wanting in them, because they still maintain some form
of relationship with Jesus Christ and His Church, and so the light
of the divine grace of the Church in some way still enlightens them.

Thus, those outside the Orthodox Church can be considered
as dwelling, after their departure from the Lord's House and from
His courts, more or less afar off.[48]

Taking all this into account, it may be said that all who fervently
seek the revealed Truth and salvation are somehow united with
the Church which preserves this Truth, and thus may be saved.

The way to the Church is opened by love proceeding from faith;
for "the man who loves his brother dwells in light" (1 Jn 2.10),
and the light leads him to union with Christ. Consequently, to
evaluate the worth of Sacraments performed outside the Church,
apart from the criterion of faith, the Church has taken into account the presence or absence of love on the part of the believers
outside her. This explains why the same local Church has at one
time recognized, and at another time pronounced invalid and in-
effectual for salvation, the Sacraments of the same heterodox, when
considering their return into her bosom.

As the Ark of truth and Steward of divine grace, the Church,
in carefully watching over the appropriation by the faithful of the
Faith and grace in Christ, remains on the basis of exactness
(akribeia). But where it is permissible, or even advisable, . . she
uses her own discretion in administering lovingly all the means
at her disposal, with the sole objective of saving the souls of her
children and of facilitating her work in the Christian world
understood in the wider sense.

The Pastoral Criteria for Economy

This being the purpose of economy in the Orthodox Church,
there have been two poles round which its practice within the
Church has revolved:

a) The first essential element taken into account in the application of economy to Christians outside Orthodoxy is the degree of
closeness shown by them to the Faith, doctrine and sacramental
grace of the Orthodox Church.

b) The second essential element is the evaluation of their feelings towards the Orthodox Church, taking into account their past actions, favorable or at least not unfavorable to Orthodoxy; also the zeal which they have displayed—officially or on a more personal level—for their incorporation into the Body of our one, holy, catholic and apostolic (Orthodox) Church.

These criteria have always been decisive in the Orthodox Church for determining whether *akribeia* or *oikonomia* should be used with regard to those outside the Church. In ancient times, this was undoubtedly the case with all heretics or schismatics, with the straying or the fallen, depending how close or how far they were dogmatically from the Orthodox Faith. Depending, too, on the greater or lesser degrees of harm they had inflicted on the Body of the Church, she would treat them differently as circumstances demanded, acting and administering her affairs in the Name of Christ and ever applying the principles of *akribeia* or *oikonomia* in the best interests of herself and her faithful.

In so doing she used circumspection, carefully weighing up the position of those to whom she was to apply *akribeia* or *oikonomia:* this meant either recognizing their Sacraments or not, and either receiving them into her bosom or else excluding them.

Such was the policy of the Orthodox Church in regulating her attitude towards the great historic heresies and schisms of the first four centuries. *She never departed from exactness so far as the basic elements of her Faith and doctrine were concerned;* but at the same time she realized the need to guard herself from the harm and hindrance which she might suffer in her work of salvation through the continuance of the heresy or schism.

This carefully balanced determination of the Church's attitude towards those who had torn themselves away from her was dictated by purely ecclesiological reasons. It was also based on the principle that, as Saint Basil says, nothing prescribed and institutionalized has such an objective value that the strict letter of exactness must be observed every time, and never the loving attitude of economy. . . .

". . . For I am under some apprehension"—Basil the Great goes on to say—"lest, in wanting to dampen their ardor over Baptism, we impede them from being saved on account of the severity of our decision. Besides, if they accept our Baptism, we should not be displeased. For we are not bound to return them the same favor, but only to obey the strict letter *(akribeia)* of the canons. On every ground let it be enjoined that those who come to us from their Baptism be anointed in the presence of the faithful, and so approach the Sacraments."[49] This means that the early Church distinguished one basic mark (among others) which she demanded from those outside her: that they should have been baptized in the Name of the Holy Trinity.

That the ancient undivided Church also sought with all her strength to preserve the peace and unity of the Church in all her relations with those more or less distant from her, and to this purpose made lavish use of economy, is evident from the 68th Canon of the local Synod of Carthage and the confirming decision of the Quinisext Ecumenical Synod. Here the heretics in question are the African Donatists, and their reception into the Orthodox Church was made as easy as possible: "Since Africa is in great need, for the peace and prosperity of the Church, those Donatist clergy who, after correcting their opinion, desire to return to catholic unity— according to the will and judgment of the Catholic bishop who governs the Church in each place—shall be received with their honors, as it is clear was done in ancient times in regard to the same division. Examples from many and, indeed, from virtually all the Churches in Africa, . . . show this to have been the practice. Not that the synod which was convened overseas . . . should be done away with, but that it may remain in force for those who wish to come over to the Catholic Church, so as to avoid creating any cleavage on these issues."[50]

Such cases go to show that the Church recognized the right, as historical examples indicate, of acting with discretionary powers and employing economy in the wide-ranging problem of relations with the non-Orthodox and their return to Orthodoxy.

Current Praxis

In subsequent times, our Orthodox Church has made use of the same freedom, and still continues to do so. Throughout the centuries following ... the first historic heresies and schisms, the Church found herself divided time and time again into fragments and local Christian units of a distinctly historical, regional, and ethnic character. Thus, in the period following the Fourth Ecumenical Synod (Chalcedon), the venerable churches of the East came into being — confessing the same Lord, living by the same Gospel, and partaking of the apostolic succession, but, at various times, differing in their closeness to the holy Orthodox Church.

While, fundamentally, never growing cold in her love for them nor diminishing in her respect for their venerable traditions, our holy Orthodox Church has, at different times and places, varied in her attitude towards them in actual practice.[51] At times she has leaned towards the demands of *akribeia,* calling into question not only the correctness of their doctrinal teaching but also the validity of their Sacraments and even of their Baptism. ... At other times she opened wide her arms and ... love towards these Churches and 'applying the Orthodox principle of *oikonomia*' proceeded to recognize some or all of their Sacraments and—always within the limits of *oikonomia*—accepted them through ecclesiastical acts and religious ceremonies of varying degree and solemnity.

These remarks hold good also for the Roman Catholic Church. In her historical relationship with the Roman Catholic Church, our holy Orthodox Church has seen the gap between them widen over centuries, through the combination of all the well-known internal and external factors. Towards Roman Catholics, likewise, she has adopted an attitude which has varied at different times and places, even though she has always perceived their closeness in the fundamentals of faith and the economy of grace as conferred both in the Sacraments and in the apostolic succession. Thus, she has varied between the strict observance of *akribeia* and the circumspect use of *oikonomia.*

As a result, down through the centuries all the different modes of reception into Orthodoxy were tried in their case:[52] they were received by the application of the rites of Baptism; by anointing with the holy Chrism; by a fresh Confession of Faith, together with the Sacrament of repentance; by a special form of prayer, or by the postulant's simply submitting a written request or Confession of Faith. In this connection it must be stressed that this wide-ranging and varied application of *oikonomia* by the Orthodox Church was due to a change in the current appreciation within the Orthodox Church of the feelings, deeds, and actions of the other. Otherwise, the nonapplication of *oikonomia* and a return to the stricter demands of *akribeia* were a vital necessity to the Orthodox Church when threatened at various times and places.

For the churches and confessions stemming from the (Protestant) Reformation—the Lutherans, Calvinists and all the others, and in particular the Anglicans—and also for the 'Old Catholics,' roughly the same criteria and the same degree of economy has prevailed. Our holy Orthodox Church has defined and regulated in each region, as time and place demanded, her relations and contacts with them, in the Spirit of economy as far as it could prevail on each occasion.

All this goes to show not only that our holy Orthodox Church has possessed wide freedom for applying economy towards her brethren in Christ outside her embrace, but also that the same use of economy in Orthodoxy, applied in due measure . . . and when it is befitting, will likewise regulate the future relations of the Orthodox Church with the other Churches and confessions.

This will continue up to the time when the various local Churches and confessions come together and unite into the one, holy, catholic, and apostolic Church. But then in their relations there will no longer be in force any form of *oikonomia,* i.e., in the sense of a temporary measure for dealing with an anomalous situation. There will only be the *akribeia* of the one Faith, expressed as a single and indivisible whole in the exactness of faith and life; and this will hold in unity the one Body of Christ.

Presuppositions and Aims of the Church

It, therefore, follows that our holy Orthodox Church, conscious of the significance and importance of present-day Christianity, not only recognizes—though being herself the one, holy, catholic and apostolic Church—the ontological existence of all these Christian Churches and confessions, but also believes that all her relationships with them are founded on the quickest and most objective clarification possible of the ecclesiological question and of their doctrinal teaching as a whole.

She also recognizes that *rapprochement* with them will be brought about on terms having as their center the divine-human structure of the Church. Yet, she by no means intends to forget the existence also of the multiple pastoral responsibilities belonging to the Church of Christ, comprising her duty to preach the Gospel "unabridged," and to remove from the conscience of the faithful everywhere all manner of censure; for it is truly a scandal to the faithful that Christians are divided, since "Christ is not divided" (1 Cor 1.13).

Our holy Orthodox Church will in no way fail to apply *akribeia* to those articles of faith and sources of grace which must be upheld. Yet, she will not neglect to employ *oikonomia* wherever permissible in local contacts with those outside her—provided always that they believe in God adored in Trinity and the basic tenets of the Orthodox Faith which follow from this, remaining always within the framework of the teaching of the ancient Church, one and indivisible.

A further goal is, on the other hand, to provide a living witness to Christ and the true Faith within a secular society and a world which, for the most part, does not follow Christ and, on the other hand, to lead all to the one Lord, the one Faith, the one Baptism, the one (Eucharist) breaking of bread, the one God and Father of all (Eph 4.5-6).

Acting in this way, our Orthodox Church aims at the following positive results:

a) First and foremost, to preserve Orthodox faith and doctrine unadulterated and uninfluenced by such condescension, "in economy," to those outside her. "For there is no room for condescension in matters of Orthodox Faith; economy can only rightly be displayed where dogma is not jeopardized" (Eulogios of Alexandria.[53].

b) To assess accurately the positive aspects in the Faith and doctrine professed by those outside her, in their eccelesiological structure, sacramental grace, and eschatological hope, to the extent that they are faithful to God's Word and Gospel of salvation.

c) To eliminate: all feelings of antagonism, violence, and self-interest; all opportunism and interference in the private affairs of each Church; all mass or individual proselytism by the well-known methods of the past, all of which have proved themselves undesirable, harmful, attacking the authority of the Churches and impeding the work of union.

d) To assess in all fairness the situations created in centuries past, but also in more recent times, within Orthodoxy and outside it, involving the reception by economy of the Sacraments of other believers on the basis of the Church's canonical practice.

e) Within the bounds of economy—identified with the extreme loving kindness of the Godhead—to find ways and means of applying this economy to the contemporary situation of good relations between the Christian Churches, with a view to furthering all aspects of common life in Christ: ecclesiastical practice, worship, common prayer, theological collaboration and consultation, etc., until the efforts of all the Churches towards union have been crowned with success.

f) To act together on particular occasions, under the presuppositions accepted by the Orthodox Church and specified above, in the spirit of mutual respect, striving, and cooperating in common for the building up of all in Christ.

This conception of economy—applied in the Orthodox Church to her own children and to those outside her, and accompanied by exactness *(akribeia),* which alone is valid in matters of faith and doctrine—is a special feature of Orthodoxy. . . . Derived from Holy Scripture and Sacred Tradition, *oikonomia* takes tangible form and finds its justification in the words of the Fathers and the canons of the Church.

From the viewpoint of divine right, it extends back as far as the Apostles and our Lord, while from the viewpoint of the Christian's approach to his neighbor it constitutes the only means whereby the Church makes allowance for human weakness, and the human element finds the possibility of drawing near to the Divine.

Thus, if *akribeia* is the chief ecclesiological mark of the one, holy, catholic, and apostolic Church—where the revealed truth and ever-abounding grace of the Triune God are concerned, *oikonomia* in the Church is her peculiar prerogative, derived from Tradition. Thereby her prudence, wisdom, pastoral openness and power to make allowances—wherever applicable—reach their full expression, so that the work of man's salvation on earth may come to fulfillment and all things may be reconciled in Christ at the last day.

NOTES

[1]This section is principally derived from the Orthodox Church of Romania's PreSynodal Report, "Economy in the Orthodox Church," in *Towards the Great Council* (London, 1972), pp. 39-54 inclusive.

[2]The *Rudder,* English Edition, p. 70; Greek Edition (1841), p.34.

[3]*Letter to Michael of Belgrade,* May 1706, K. Delikanis, *Patriarchal Documents* (Constantinople 1905), 3, p. 684.

[4]See Canons 46, 47, 48 of the Holy Apostles; 3 and 4 of Saint Gregory of Nyssa; 1, 3, 10, 47 of Saint Basil the Great; *Letter of the Third Ecumenical Synod,* cf. Rallis-Potlis, *Constitution of the Sacred and Holy Canons,* Vols. 3, 2, 4, and 2.

[5]See Canons 2 and 5 of Ankyra; 11 and 12 of the First Ecumenical Synod; 2 and 5 of Saint Gregory of Nyssa; 3, 5, 10, 17, 18, etc. of Saint Basil; 2 of Saint Cyril of Alexandria; 16 of the Fourth Ecumenical Synod; 3, 29, 30, 102 of the Sixth Ecumenical Synod, etc. in Rallis-Potlis, Vols. 3, 2, 4, and 2.

[6]See Canons 7 and 8 of the First Ecumenical Synod, 7 of the Second Ecumenical Synod; 1 and 47 of Saint Basil; Sixth Ecumenical Synod, cf. Rallis-Potlis, Vols. 2, 4.

[7]Cf. Saint Clement of Alexandria, *Stromateis* 1, 17; PG 8.800-01 and Saint Cyril of Alexandria, *Letters,* 41; PG 77.217.

[8]Tertullian, *Against Praxeas 2;* Saint Basil, *Letters,* 2nd Series, 189, 7; PG 32.693.

[9]Saint Clement of Alexandria, *Stromateis* 1, 17, PG 8.800-01.

[10]*Ibid., 7, 12, PG 9.501; Andrew of Caesarea in Cappadocia, Commentary on the Apocalypse,* PG 106.385.

[11]Saint Athanasios the Great, *Letters to Serapion,* 4, 14, PG 26.656; Saint Basil, *On the Holy Spirit,* 16, 39, PG 32.140; Saint Cyril of Alexandria, "varia" in PG 76.16, 17, 40, 148, 209, 212, 300, 301, 304, 320, 341, 417, 424, 1177, 1185, 1340, 1388 and PG 77.16, 132 etc.; Saint Maximos the Confessor, *On Theology and the Economy of the Son's Incarnation,* 18, 23, PG 90.1133, 1136; Saint John of Damascus, *An Exact Exposition of the Orthodox Faith,* 3, 1, *On the Divine Economy,* 1, 2, 5, 12, 17, 28, PG 94.981, 988, 1000, 1069, 1100; Saint Photios, *Amphilochia,* quest. 1, 61, 14, PG 101.48, 64-65; Id. *Bibliotheca,* 227, 230, etc., PG l03.953, 1025, 1028.

[12]Saint Clement of Alexandria, *Stromateis* 2, 5; PG 8.952; Saint Gregory of Nazianzos and Constantinople, Sermon 38, 14; PG 36.329.

[13]Saint Athanasios, *Commentary on the 67th Psalm,* PG 27.300; Saint Cyril of Alexandria, *Against Nestorios,* 1, 4; PG 76.40, *Exegesis of the 12 Anathemas,* 2, 3, 4; PG 76.300, 301, 304; *Defense of the 12 Anathemas against Theodoret;* PG 77.417, 424, 425; Saint Anastasios of Sinai, *On the Economy,* 1, PG 89.85.

[14]Saint Cyril of Alexandria, *On the Trinity,* 26; PG 77.1169; Saint John of Damascus, *Exposition of the Orthodox Faith,* 3, 2, 3, 5, 3, 17; PG 94.988, 1032, 1069, etc.; Saint Photios, *Amphilochia,* 14; PG 101.65.

[15]Saint Basil, *Letters,* 2nd Series, 243, l; PG 32.904, 245, 3; PG 32.989; Saint Photios, *Bibliotheca,* 227; PG 103.953, 956; Canon 1, Sixth Ecumenical Synod.

[16]Mansi 13, 129.

[17]Mansi 12, 1010, 1038ff.

[18]See Canons 2, and 5 of Ankyra with the commentaries of Zonaras and Balsamon, Rallis-Potlis, Vol. 3, pp. 23, 32 and Vol. 4, p. 33. See also comments of Aristenos on Canon 5 of Ankyra; Canons 11 and 12 of First Ecumenical Synod, the latter with comments of Aristenos, in Rallis-Potlis, Vol. 2, p. 143; Canons 1, 3, and 10 of Saint Basil; Canon 29 of Sixth Ecumenical Synod; Matthew Blastares, *Constitution,* section M, chapter 7, in Rallis-Potlis, Vol. 6, pp. 364-66.

[19]See Canons 3 and 10 of Saint Basil, 3 and 4 of Saint Gregory of Nyssa, 15 of the Fourth Ecumenical Synod, 3 and 29 of Sixth Ecumenical Synod, 102 of Sixth Ecumenical Synod.

[20]Saint Basil, *On the Holy Spirit,* chapter 17, 39; PG 32.140; Saint Cyril of Alexandria, *Against Nestorios,* 1, i, 4ff.; PG 76.16, 17, 40ff.

[21]Saint Cyril of Alexandria, *On the Holy Trinity,* 14; PG 77.1149; Theodotos of Ancyra, *On the Nicene Creed,* 2, 5, 7; PG 77.1317, 1320, 1324; Saint Maximos the Confessor, *200 Chapters,* 2nd century, 18; PG 90.1133; Saint Anastasios of Sinai, *On the Economies,* 1; PG 89.85; Saint John of Damascus, *Exposition of the Orthodox Faith,* 3, i; PG 94.984.

[22]*Letters to Serapion,* 4, 14; PG 26.656, 26.39; *Commentary on Psalms 67 and 71;* PG 27.300, 325.

[23]*On the Holy Spirit,* 8, 18; PG 32.100, 140.

[24]*Against Nestorios,* 1, 3, 5; PG 76.16, 17, 40, 148, 209, 212, and *Exegesis of the 12 Anathemas and Defense of the 12 Anathemas;* PG 36.300, 301, 304, 320ff.

[25]*On the Nicene Creed,* 2, 5, 7, 8, 18, 20, 21, 22ff; PG 77.1317, 1324, 1345ff.

[26]*200 Chapters,* 2nd century, 23, 24; PG 90.1136.

[27]*Exposition of the Orthodox Faith,* 2, 2, 5, 13, 17, 18; PG 94.988, 1000, 1032ff.

[28]*Amphilochia,* quest. 1, 14, 43, 13, 14, 16; PG 101.63, 320, 321, 325, 932.

[29]See Canon 1.

[30]See Canon 102 of the Quinisext Ecumenical Synod.

[31]Canons 1-4 and 6-8.

[32]PG 49.405, 408 and 61.640.

[33]PG 77.248, 249, 300, 320, 321, 344, 345, 349, 353, 376.

[34]PG 77.1317, 1320, 1324ff.

[35]Rallis-Potlis, Vol. 4, 423-46.

[36]PG 86.2, 2940 and PG 103.953-56.

[37]PG 90.1133, 1136.

[38]PG 89.85.

[39]Rallis-Potlis, Vol. 4, 427ff and PG 100.377-93.

[40]PG 99.1072-1084.

[41]PG 101.64 and PG 102.773, 776; PG 103.953-56, 1025, 1028.

[42]PG 111.212, 213.

[43]Rallis-Potlis, Vol. 2, 210, 257, 367, 369, 551-52; Vol. 3, 23, 32; Vol. 4, 93, 100, 211, 311-12.

[44]Ibid., Vol. 2, 213-14, 368, 370, 553; vol. 3, 23; vol. 4, 101, 312-14.

[45]Ibid., Vol. 2, 142-43; vol. 3, 33; vol. 4, 94, 199-211.

[46]PG 111.212-13.

[47]Rallis-Potlis, Vol. 2, 552-54.

[48]Saint Photios, *Bibliotheca,* 227; PG 103.953-56.

[49]Rallis-Potlis, Vol. 4, 91-2.

[50]Rallis-Potlis, Vol. 3, 476.

[51]E.g., a leading mystical teacher of the ancient (Nestorian) Church of the East, Saint Isaac of Nineveh (Syria), is universally celebrated throughout the Orthodox Church and her ecclesiastical writings as a worthy spiritual father-confessor and 'model' for emulation not only by monastics and hermits, but likewise by those 'in the world' who seek 'the interior way.' See: *Early Fathers from the Philokalia: Together with Some Writings of Saint Abba Dorotheos, Saint Isaac of Syria and Saint*

Gregory Palamas, trans. E. Kadloubovsky and G. E. H. Palmer (London, 1954), and *Writings from the Philokalia On Prayer of the Heart,* idem, (London, 1957).

[52]See: "The Reception of Roman Catholics into Orthodoxy: Historical Variations and Norms," by Bishop Peter (L'Huillers) of New York, *St. Vladimir's Theological Quarterly,* 24 (1980) 75-82.

[53]PG 103.953.

CHAPTER SEVEN:

Orthodox Ecumenical Witness in the Twentieth Century

The scriptural, patristic, and conciliar witness across the ages amply demonstrates that there is no need, justification, or excuse for the Orthodox Church either to act as "an unwilling and reluctant partner in the [modern] ecumenical enterprise," or for the "sociopsychological climate in Orthodoxy [to be] reserved about ecumenism."[1] Despite the fact that the most vigorous twentieth-century "inspiration and initial impulse . . . came from Protestant sources,"[2] the fact remains that—historically, theologically, and canonically—both the evangelical mission and *oikonomia* of ecumenism are properly the living heritage of the Orthodox Catholic Church and central to her very being and self-understanding. She must initiate and creatively pursue ecumenical action, not just react.

No one has realized this fact of life more than the modern ecumenical pioneers of the holy Ecumenical Patriarchate and the Church of Russia. Both, almost from the inception of this era, have had to operate under conditions of severe restraint, or have even been held captive by hostile forces and unfriendly outside groups. Yet, despite such handicaps, they continue to sustain a faithful continuum of ecumenical witness and activity. Viewing the tatters of war-torn Europe and the bold sociopolitical effort towards unity known as the "League of Nations," the Ecumenical Patriarchate saw and seized upon the opportunity to begin a like effort among the churches and confessional communions of Christendom. Those who dare to bear the one Name of Christ, the bishops reasoned, ought to "no longer trail piteously after the politicians," who had acted "for the defense of right and the cultivation of love and harmony among the nations."[3] In fact, the first modern encyclical on the need and potential of Christian ecumenism came, in 1902, from the prayers and pen of the Ecumenical Patriarch, Joachim III, acting in common council with his brethren of the Holy Synod of

Constantinople.

The best proof "that there has been no fundamental alteration in the ecumenical and ecclesiological principles of Orthodoxy" is the actual articulation in this century of the Church's authentic ecumenical Tradition, as viewed and set forth by some of her leading contemporary spokesmen.

The Basic Charter: "Unto All the Churches of Christ . . ."

> "See that you love one another,
> with a pure heart and fervently." (1 Pet 1.22)

Our Church is persuaded that a closer relationship and a mutual understanding among the several Christian Churches is not hindered by their doctrinal differences . . . is both desirable and necessary, indeed is in the best interests of the Churches, both individually and as the whole Body of Christ. It will prepare and facilitate that perfect, blessed union which, with God's help, may one day be realized. . . . For while ancient prejudices, traditions and even pretensions, which have in the past frustrated the work of unity, may even now raise difficulties, nevertheless it is better to [face] them. If there be goodwill and good intent, they neither can nor ought to prove insuperable obstacles.[4]

If this should be impossible with men, as in the case in every thing, it is nevertheless possible with God. . . . With the aid of divine grace which cooperates with persons who walk in the paths of evangelical love and peace, . . . [we may find] similarities and points of contact, or even mutual controverted points [which were] previously overlooked, up to that moment when the entire task is completed and the prayer of our Lord and God and Savior Jesus Christ is fulfilled, for the common joy and benefit of the one flock and the one Shepherd.[5]

Brethren! . . . together with you, the representatives of other Christian Churches . . . we bewail the rending of the seamless robe of Christ. We desire, as you, that the members of the one Body of Christ may again be reunited, and we pray . . . in our congregations for the union of all humankind.[6]

With sincerity and mutual confidence thus restored among the Churches, we believe that charity, too, must be revived and deepened, so that they will no longer regard one another as strangers, enemies even, but as relatives and friends in Christ, "fellow heirs, members of the same Body, and partakers of the promise in Christ Jesus through the Gospel" (Eph 3.6).

By promoting a constant brotherly concern for the conditions, the stability, and the well-being of the other Churches; by their eagerness to know what is happening in those Churches and by acquiring a more accurate knowledge of them; by their readiness, whenever the occasion arises, to offer the helping hand, [thus] will they accomplish much good, to their own credit and profit and that of the whole Christian Body, and to further the cause of unity. . . .

For today's dangers no longer threaten a particular Church, [but] rather all of them together, attacking as they do the very foundations of Christian Faith and the very composition of Christian life and society. . . . All these things present the gravest dangers to the constitution of Christian society. . . . The questions of the day call for common study and cooperation on the part of the Christian Churches.

Finally, it is the duty of the Churches, graced with the sacred Name of Christ, no longer to forget and neglect his "New Commandment," the Great Commandment of love. . . .[7] In opposition to the anti-Christian tendencies in the world . . . the task of *rapprochement* and cooperation between all the Christian confessions and organizations is a sacred obligation and a holy duty, derived from their function and mission.[8]

We request each one to make known to us in reply its own thoughts and beliefs concerning this matter. Once we have by consensus and agreement defined the objective, we may safely proceed together toward its realization, and thus, "speaking the truth in love, we grow up in every way into Him Who is the Head, into Christ, from Whom the whole Body, joined and knit together by every joint with which it is supplied, when each part is working properly, makes bodily growth and upbuilds itself in love" (Eph 4.15).[9]

The Nature of the Church and the Unity We Seek

The holy Church, we say, is truly one . . . and indeed she must be one: not many and contrary Churches, differing from one another in dogmas and the fundamental institutions of ecclesiastical order. . . .[10]

Agreement cannot be reached by vague phrases, or by a compromise of antithetical opinions.[11] We Orthodox . . . stress the necessity of accuracy and concreteness in the formulation of the Faith and . . . that ambiguous expressions and comprehensive expressions of the Faith are of no real value [when] used to identify conceptions and tenets that actually are different from one another.[12]

Thus, for example, we cannot conceive how agreement can be made possible between two . . . which agree that the existence of the ministry of the Church is by the will of Christ, yet differ as to whether that ministry was in fact instituted by Christ. . . . For, according to the Orthodox Church, where the wholeness of Faith is absent, there can be no *communio in sacris.* Nor can we here apply that principle of *oikonomia* which in the past the Orthodox Church has applied under quite other circumstances in the case of those who came to her with a view to union. . . .[13]

We would not pass judgment on those of the separated communions [wherein] certain basic elements are lacking which constitute the reality of the fullness of the Church. But we believe that the return of these communions to the Faith of the ancient, united, and indivisible Church of the Seven Ecumenical Synods, the pure and unchanged and common heritage of the forefathers of all divided Christians, shall alone produce the desired reunion of all separated Christians.

For only the unity and the fellowship of Christians in common faith shall have as a necessary result their fellowship in the Sacraments . . . as members of the one and the same Body of the one Church of Christ. . . .

Nor can the Orthodox Church accept that the Holy Spirit speaks to us only through the Bible. The Holy Spirit abides and witnesses through the wholeness, the totality of the Church's life and experience. The Bible is given to us within the context of Apostolic

Tradition, in which, in turn, we possess the authentic interpretation and explication of the Word of God . . . safeguarding the reality
and continuity of church unity. . . .[14]

The Church, and not . . . the written and preached Word [is]
primary in the work of our salvation. It is by the Church that the
Scriptures are given to us. . . .[15]

It is necessary, therefore, to place an adequate emphasis on
the actual presence of the Kingdom of God, in the Church.[16] The
Kingdom has been founded by God through the incarnation of
his Son, the redemption, the resurrection, the ascension of Christ
in glory, and the descent of the Holy Spirit.

The Kingdom has been existing on earth since Pentecost
and is open to all persons, bestowing — to all who enter — the
power which transforms and renews human existence now on
earth.

Life eternal is not only an object of future realization: it is given to those who were called by the Word of God in the Sacrament of Baptism (Rom 6) and is continuously renewed through
the participation in the Holy Eucharist. God has left nothing undone for . . . the immediate transformation of human existence.
Thus, our participation in the renewed life of the Kingdom of God
is a present reality as well as a future fulfillment.[17]

It is through the Apostolic ministry that the mystery of Pentecost
is perpetuated in the Church. The episcopal succession from the
Apostles constitutes an historical reality in the life and structure
of the Church, one of the presuppositions of her unity throughout
the ages.[18] That ministry [was] instituted by Christ Himself in its
three degrees of bishop, presbyter, and deacon.[19] The unity of the
Church is preserved through the unity of the episcopate . . .
safeguarded by the common Faith arising spontaneously out of
the fullness (*pleroma*) of the Church.[20]

Of all the promises of Christ, the most precious is the one in
which He asserts that the Holy Trinity will abide in us (Jn 14.23,
15.26, 16.13-17, 17.21-26) . . . [and] the Orthodox Church gives
clear expression to this truth in one of her prayers: "My hope is
in the Father; my refuge is the Son; my comfort, my shelter is the
Holy Spirit: O Holy Trinity, glory to Thee."

The power of God is indeed operating in the midst of human

weakness. We can never fulfill all the demands which Christ makes upon us: in humility and repentance, we must acknowledge our limitations and shortcomings, . . . yet it is in the Church that we find this strength. The reality of the New Life is never annulled or compromised by our own failures. Thus, the Church of Christ, as the realized Kingdom of God, lies beyond judgment; whereas her members, being liable to sin and error, are subject to the Judgment.[21] We reject the idea that the Church herself, being the Body of Christ and the repository of revealed truth and the "whole operation of the Holy Spirit" . . . which is intrinsically holy and unerring, [could ever] be repentant. For, "Christ loved the Church and gave Himself for her, that He might sanctify her in the washing of the water and the Word, that He might present her to Himself as a glorious Church, not having spot or wrinkle or blemish or any such thing, but that she should be holy and without blemish" (Eph 5.26-27).

Thus, the Lord, the only Holy One, sanctified His Church forever and ordained that her task be the "edification of the Saints, the building of the Body of Christ."[22]

Orthodoxy's Special Responsibility

The Orthodox Church feels that, since she was not associated with the events related to the breakdown of religious unity in the West, she bears a special responsibility to contribute to the restoration of Christian unity, which alone can render the message of the Gospel effective in a troubled world. . . .[23]

For the Orthodox, the basic ecumenical problem is that of schism . . . [so we] cannot accept the idea of a "parity of denominations" [or] visualize Christian reunion just as an interdenominational adjustment.[24]

It is with humility that . . . the Orthodox Church is always prepared to meet with Christians of other communions in inter-confessional deliberations [and] ecumenical conversations that aim at removing the barriers to Christian unity.[25]

The common background of existing denominations can be found and must be sought in . . . that common, ancient and Apostolic Tradition from which all derive existence. . . . The report of Faith and Order itself mentions "agreement [in faith] with all ages" as one of the normative prerequisites of unity [and] this new method of ecumenical inquiry, a new criterion of ecumenical evaluation, [offers] the hope that unity may be recovered by the divided denominations by their return to their common past.

The Orthodox Church is willing to participate in this common work as the witness which has preserved continuously[26] . . . the Tradition of the ancient, undivided Church . . . in an unbroken and continuous succession of sacramental ministry. . . .[27] It pleases God to preserve "his treasure in earthen vessels, that the excellency of the power may be of God" (2 Cor 4.7).[28]

No static restoration of old forms is anticipated, . . . nor should there be a rigid uniformity, since the same Faith—mysterious in its essence and unable to be fathomed adequately by formulas of human reason—can be expressed accurately in different manners. . . . [Rather] the immediate objective of the ecumenical search is, according to the Orthodox understanding, a reintegration of Christian mind, recovery of Apostolic Tradition, a fullness of Christian vision and belief, in agreement with all ages.[29]

The general reunion of Christian Churches may possibly be hastened if union is first achieved between those Churches which present features of great similarity with one another. In such a way, the gradual drawing together of the Christian churches may be helped and promoted.[30] The happy results which have now been reached in different parts of Christendom [towards this limited end and the ultimate goal] fill us with hope and give us encouragement to continue our efforts in the direction of an ultimate reunion of all Christians.[31]

Particular Ecumenical Principles in Practice

The Role of Inter-Church Councils

According to the constitution of the World Council of Churches, it is its function:

*to facilitate common action by the Churches,

*to promote cooperation in the study of the Christian spirit,

*to promote the growth of the ecumenical consciousness in the members of all the Churches,
*to support the distribution of the sacred Gospel, and
*to preserve, uplift, and cause to prevail the spiritual values of man, in the most general Christian context. . . .

[For these reasons] we consider that, in many ways, the future participation and cooperation of the Orthodox Church with the World Council of Churches is necessary. . . . The individual sister Churches [of holy Orthodoxy] should cooperate appropriately in the common study and preparation of the subjects to be considered in the assemblies of the World Council of Churches, so that our Church [might act] in pan-Christian conferences . . . with the strength and authority appropriate to her position and to her historic mission in the world. . . . [32]

A very real unity has been discovered in ecumenical meetings; this is, to all who collaborate in the World Council, the most precise element of its life . . . as an unmerited gift from the Lord. We praise God for this foretaste of the unity of His people and continue hopefully with the work to which He has called us together, . . . [33] [for] a converging of minds has been demonstrated indeed in discussions on the nature of the Church, Tradition, and worship.[34]

The past quarter century has been equally enriching for Orthodoxy, both in the area of interchurch experience and theological study, and in the area of concrete and generous manifestations of Christian charity and mutual assistance, which have placed Christ in the hearts of millions of distressed Christians and many of our afflicted fellow human beings. All these things . . . are continuing to contribute to the opening of hearts in a Christ-beloved interpretation of the Christian Churches and confessions that confess the same Lord. . . .

However, as an institution [the World Council] unquestionably has within itself all the presuppositions and the power of self-development, [so] it also undergoes moments of crisis and self-examination which the Ecumenical Patriarchate and the whole of Orthodoxy, despite their great confidence in the Council, follows with careful attention in the present moment of ecumenism.

As is well-known, the World Council . . . is now inclining towards new areas. . . . Naturally, the problems of our sick society are also [the World Council's] own problems, as well as [being] the problems of individual Christian churches. . . . Indeed, the World Council of Churches feels compelled to assume the responsibility for extending its efforts towards all of these new and ever increasing realities.

However, the question is raised: is it possible that all these issues, and only these, constitute the object and sole orientation of the World Council? . . . The question is fundamental . . . expressing the deeper crisis currently rocking the ecumenical movement and the World Council of Churches as such. . . .

The relevant views of the Ecumenical Patriarchate on the matter [are as follows]:

> The World Council of Churches is and should remain a "Council of Churches" in accordance with the express requirements [of] . . . its constitution, . . .[including the ministry] to serve the Churches in their broader efforts toward unity and cooperation within a fractured humankind [which] still seminally contains the essential unity of the human race. . . .
>
> As an institution dedicated to the service of the Churches, the World Council is obligated to act as the specific organ of the Churches in their common search for the shaken and elusive unity of the Churches, both in the manifestation of the common signs of grace, truth, and faith entrusted to them and in the investigation and resolution of existing differences. . . .
>
> Furthermore, it should weigh the reasons why contemporary man is repelled by certain aspects of the Churches and their theology, so that it may discover the most appropriate means of expressing Christian *didache* and . . . not the insignificant word of a secularized movement, like so many

others, . . . but rather a proclamation rich in prophetic tone, the very Word of Christ. . . .

In fulfilling its basic aims, the World Council is bound to test all the theological insights, ranging from ecumenical dialogue to the candid presentation of the Faith and doctrine of participating members with full theological honesty and integrity, so that from the plurality of their teachings, the oneness of the revealed truth in Christ may be distilled from both Holy Scriptures and sacred Tradition upon which alone would be based any form of desired unity by the Council. . . .[35]

The purpose of the World Council is not to negotiate unions between Churches, which can only be done by the Churches themselves acting on their own initiative, but to bring the Churches into living contact with each other and to promote the study and discussion of the issues of Church unity. . . . In no case can or will any Church be pressed to take any decision against its own conviction or desire. . . . [36]

Local and Regional Ecumenism[37]

Ecumenical assemblies of various kinds have become . . . meaningful. Programs of dialogue, such as panels, interfaith forums and convocations, open house programs, etc., are desirable ways of improving understanding across confessional lines . . . arranged through local councils of Churches or ministerial associations or existing interfaith committees. . . . The effort should be made to reflect the mind of the Church through the use of published sources of its theologians and leaders, [for] to engage profitably in dialogue, it is essential that we know the Orthodox position thoroughly. . . .

The term "dialogue" means nothing more nor less than Christian conversation. . . . Love grows out of knowing one another. Essential, therefore, to dialogue is the fullest possible knowledge and understanding of those with whom we are engaged in conversation. . . .

Local ecumenism, ultimately the only real ecumenism, must

involve the laity as well. . . . Therefore, the [dioceses and] parishes are urged to undertake a far more serious program of education, both in Orthodox Faith and practice and in comparative religion, than has been the norm, [for] it is equally imperative that [the Orthodox] be well rooted in Orthodox Faith and practice, before they attempt to interpret them to others or defend them. . . .

For the purposes of acquiring a deeper knowledge and understanding of the beliefs and practices of others, [Orthodox] may . . . attend official worship in other Churches—especially as part of regular religious education programs. . . .

The experience of sincere Christian people in the local community forms the soundest base for the whole ecumenical development. One of the primary benefits, even without that final unity for which Christ prayed, is the freedom of all Christian bodies to labor together for the general good of society. And such cooperation can be very vital and real at the local level, where the common problems and concerns are many: education, public welfare, racial tensions, urban renewal, unemployment.

If *koinonia* in the fullest sense is difficult for us to realize, indeed even to define adequately, at this stage of our ecumenical maturity, yet *diakonia* can and should unite us. The councils of Churches, at the local level, are an appropriate and desirable means for achieving such cooperation. They represent a long tradition and rich experience in coordinating the activities of the Churches, particularly in the area of civic and social witness and service.[38]

Individual Orthodox Christians, of course, are obliged to assist in every effort or activity which embodies justice, the principles of brotherhood, and which provides more favorable conditions for the spiritual development of both personality and community.[39]

Ecumenical Worship[40]

When the Lord declares, "Where two or three are gathered in my name, there am I in the midst of them" (Mt 18.20), there is no inference of fellowship only within confessional boundaries. So, when we join our otherwise separated brothers in common supplication, it is an expression of our being bound together by those "ties which God has not yet willed to reveal to us."[41]

"Ecumenical services" refer to forms of [non-covenantal] worship or devotion mutually acceptable to all participating parties in which Christians of various communions take part. Although such services are concerned particularly with the restoration of Christian unity, they may be held for any common concern in which Christians can and should cooperate with one another.

"Ecumenical services" may be conducted in an Orthodox Church with the permission of the bishop. Furthermore, Orthodox Christians may take part in such services in the Churches of other communions. . . [if] publicly acknowledged and identified as "ecumenical" in character, emphasizing the firm Orthodox position that these are prayers for unity, and not . . . Eucharistic celebration. . . .

Although petitions and prayers for unity are a regular part of the Orthodox liturgical practice [from the earliest centuries], "ecumenical services" may be encouraged as a means of sensitizing our faithful to the tragedy of Christian disunity and of developing the spirit of charity, understanding, and prayer for all. . . .

Unity in the Faith and the active life of the community is a necessary precondition to sharing in the Sacraments of the Orthodox Church. . . . "To the Holy Communion the Church admits only her baptized and chrismated children who confess the full Orthodox Faith, pure and entire, and by it she shows forth their oneness with her and with her divine Spouse (Jesus Christ). Holy Communion is the sign and evidence of right belief and of incorporation in the Israel of God. . . ."

The intimate relation of the Sacraments to the community of Faith and grace precludes the participation of non-Orthodox in their celebration [as communicants.][42] . . . Intercommunion must be considered as the crowning act of a real and true reunion which has already been fully achieved by fundamental agreement in the realm of Faith and Order, and is not to be regarded as an instrument for reunion.[43]

Formal liturgical worship (sacramental communion and celebration) . . . of clergy and laity of different confessions is contrary to the canons of the Orthodox Church . . . [as it projects] a false impression of the Christian Faith and the nature of the unity which

God has given to those in His Church. . . . [It is] a false presentation before the heavenly Altar of God.[44]

There are, indeed, real difficulties here that ought honestly
to be faced. And in facing them and identifying them, we can help
to make clear a basic Orthodox position: that unity at the Altar
(*communicatio in sacris*) must be seen as the ultimate fruit of our
labors and of our painful unity efforts, but not the means to that
unity.[45]

Miscellany

Our Church is not made up of walls and roofs, but rather of
life and faith (The Pan-Orthodox Presynodal Conference at Rhodes,
1961).

We repudiate the theme that all religions are equally valid,
because it flattens diversities and ignores contradictions. It not
only obscures the meaning of the Christian Faith, but also fails
to respect the integrity of other faiths.

Truth *does* matter: therefore, differences among religions are
deeply significant ("The Hartford Appeal," January, 1975).

Whatever else may be written about the century in which we
live, history will regard as one of its dominant themes the
"ecumenical movement." It will record that Christianity exhausted
its centrifugal forces which brought about its divisions and set out
in an earnest quest for its lost unity.

It is central to our Faith that *Christ is not divided.* . . . And
as it is not given to us fully to know the nature of the inner Oneness
of Father and Son, so we may not fully comprehend the nature
of the Church's inner Oneness.

This, then, is the essence of the ecumenical movement: a desire
to know God's will for His Church . . . undertaken in faith, in obedience, and with a willingness to respond affirmatively to the
urgings of the Holy Spirit.

The ecumenical vocation is addressed to the Orthodox Church
no less than to the others. For, *though we know where the Church
is,* as a modern Orthodox thinker has put it, *we cannot be sure
where the Church is not* (Greek Orthodox Archbishop Iakovos of
America, 1966).

Master, in this hour stand in the midst of us all. Purify our hearts and sanctify our souls, and cleanse us from all sins that we have done willingly or unwillingly. Grant us to offer to Thee reasonable oblations and right praise, a spiritual sweet savour, that we may enter in within the Holy of Holies.

Remember, O Lord, the peace of Thy one, holy, catholic, and apostolic Church, which is from one end of the world to the other.

(Coptic Liturgy of Saint Mark).

NOTES

[1]Robert G. Stephanopoulos, *Guidelines,* p. 2.

[2]Ibid.

[3]1920 Encyclical of the Ecumenical Patriarchate, p. 29.

[4]Ibid., p. 27.

[5]1902 Encyclical of the Ecumenical Patriarchate, p. 26.

[6]1937 "Declaration on Behalf of the Eastern Orthodox Church," at Second Faith & Order Conference, Edinburgh, p. 38.

[7]1920 Encyclical, pp. 28-29.

[8]1952 Encyclical of Ecumenical Patriarch Athenagoras I, p. 39.

[9]1920 Encyclical, p. 29.

[10]1902 Encyclical, p. 26.

[11]1927 "Declaration . . ." at First Faith & Order Conference, Lausanne, p. 33.

[12]1937 "Declaration," Edinburgh, p. 37.

[13]1927 "Declaration," Lausanne, p. 33.

[14]1954 "Declaration Concerning Faith and Order," Evaston, p.46.

[15]1937 "Declaration," Evanston, p. 36.

[16]This is basically the reason why the eucharistic Divine Liturgy and every major sacramental celebration of the Eastern Orthodox Church begin with the proclamation in faith: "Blessed is the Kingdom of the Father, and of the Son, and of the Holy Spirit, now and ever, and unto ages of ages. Amen."

[17]1954 "Statement on the Main Theme: 'Christ, the Hope of the World,'" Evanston, p. 43.

[18]1954 "Declaration," Evanston, p. 46.

[19]1927 "Declaration," Lausanne, p. 33.

[20]1954 "Declaration," Evanston, p. 46.

[21]1954 "Statement," Evanston, pp. 43-44.

[22]1954 "Declaration," Evanston, p. 47.

[23]1957 "Statement of the Eastern Orthodox Churches in the U.S.A.," Oberlin, p. 49.

[24]1961 "Contribution: the Section on Unity," Assembly of the World Council of Churches, New Delhi, p. 50.

[25]1957 "Statement," Oberlin, p. 49.

[26]1961 "Contribution," New Delhi, p. 51.

[27]Ibid., p. 50.

[28]1954 "Declaration," Evanston, p. 47.

[29]1961 "Contribution," New Delhi, p. 51.

[30]1937 "Declaration," Oxford, p. 37.

[31]Ibid., pp. 37-38.

[32]1952 Patriarchal Encyclical, pp. 39-41.

[33]1950 World Council of Churches' Statement, "The Church, the Churches, and the World Council of Churches," Assembly at Toronto, p. 63.

[34]John S. Romanides, *Arrival and Dialogue* (New York, 1964), p. 18.

[35]1973 "Message of the Ecumenical Patriarchate: To the World Council of Churches on Its 25th Anniversary," Constantinople and Geneva; in Stephanopoulos, *Guidelines*, pp. 54-60.

[36]1950 World Council of Churches' Statement, Toronto, pp. 62-63.

[37]The above is but an overview of the general and particular principles of Orthodox ecumenical practice. More detailed and particular guidelines, in particular of the Orthodox Churches in the Americas, must be sought from the chancery of the particular Orthodox jurisdiction and that Church's local bishop.

[38]Leonidas Contos, *Guidelines for the Orthodox in Ecumenical Relations* (New York, 1966).

[39]Stephanopoulos, *Guidelines,* p. 12.

[40]See note 37 above.

[41]Contos, *Guidelines.* In opposition to "ecumenical worship" and common prayer of any sort among divided Christians, which is observed generally by Orthodox Churches, certain traditionalists appeal to the unequivocal prohibition thereof which is contained in the so-called "85 Apostolic Canons." But proponents of limited, noncovenantal "ecumenical services" and common prayer make three observations, contesting this interpretation of the Church's *consensus fidelium.* First, the date, origin, intent, and *situs* for these canons are still unknown. Secondly, their anti-ecumenical spirit is, scripturally speaking, a minority position, not supported by the example of the Lord and His disciples. Third, in several major respects they are apparently annulled by the acts of Ecumenical and major Regional Synods, beginning with Nicaea I, as well as in the pastoral practice of various noted Fathers during the Church's first millenium.

[42]Stephanopoulos, *Guidelines,* p. 12.

[43]1937 "Declaration," Edinburgh, p. 37.
Many perceive the basic requirements for communion among certain canonically separated churches as fulfilled, "in practical unity." They urge the Church, by *oikonomia,* to allow for a gradual growing back together "existentially" within a basic state of unity, to be extended even before the final details of organic reunion are to be reached among the Eastern Orthodox, the ancient Churches of the East, the "Old Catholic" and Roman Catholic Churches. They appeal to the "precedent" of the partially unsettled state of organic union, yet communion which existed (after the Council of Reunion, A.D. 879-80) between the Orthodox and Roman Catholic Churches, respectively under the leadership of Pope John VIII and Patriarch Photios I. For variations and commentaries on this proposal for a "limited relaxation" of the strict canonical principle, see *Communion and Intercommunion,* Kallistos (Timothy) Ware (Minneapolis, 1980), and "The One Church and the Churches," *The Thyateira Confession: The Faith and Prayer of the People of God,* by the late Archbishop Athenagoras (Kokkinakis) of Thyateira and Great Britain (London, 1975), pp. 78-79.

[44]"Christian Unity and Ecumenism," in *Documents of the Orthodox Church in America,* March, 1973.

[45]Contos, *Guidelines.*

EPILOGUE:

Reflections and Taking Stock

Despite misgivings and even opposition in some quarters, the modern ecumenical movement has had a profound effect on the Church. This is true especially of Eastern Orthodoxy and Roman Catholicism. As encounter with one another and with others has increased over the years, the two separated sister communions have begun gradually to shed their exclusively "Eastern/Byzantine" and "Roman/Western" characters. They are being challenged to resume once again in history their common Orthodox Catholic witness to a diverse but united church of Christ.

There is also a realization of crisis which even catastrophic revolutions and two major world wars were not quite able to produce. It is that Christians and authentic Christian values, whether "Eastern" or "Roman" or "Reformed," are fast becoming the minority in the contemporary worlds in which we live. These are: a Western world increasingly dominated by secular, humanist, and neo-pagan value systems; unfree "socialist" commonwealths in Eastern Europe and Asia, and an array of similarly unfree nations in Latin America and Africa where crushing poverty, militarism, remnants of former colonialisms, and neo-tribalism demean the human spirit; and a "Third World" wherein the adherents of non-Christian religions and values are the more numerous. A divided Christendom can hardly make the encounter with such an *oikoumene* a fruitful one, or otherwise meet the challenge these factors present, and certainly not in the spirit with which the early Church Fathers did so. A sense of urgency is in order, many Christians feel, and a sectarian, or "ghetto," Christianity can only fail far worse than did the warring, divided Church in the encounter with the Renaissance and the Enlightenment.

Fortunately, Christianity has an inner vitality and resilience unmatched in the gamut of world religions. To an extent genuine convergence, humanitarian concern, and a search for roots are beginning to take hold once again within contemporary Christendom.[1] No doubt, as Ecumenical Patriarch Demetrios and the

"Metropolia" Orthodox Church in America[2] observed in their respective 1973 synodal encyclicals, some movements and individual leaders do see Christian unity less in terms of a holy consensus of Apostolic communion restored in integrity, and more so in terms of glossing over historic issues, of "intercommunion" among individuals and loosely-defined confessional denominations and alliances, and of "the world setting the Church's agenda." The patristic vision of the Church is neither popular nor universally appreciated.

After nearly twenty years of individual and professional involvement, I have come personally to view the contemporary ecumenical movement, whatever its drawbacks and failings, as an inexorable process leading towards Christian unity. As this study has indicated, it is a key evangelical imperative that is integral to the Church's inner being. The rapid growth of serious bilateral dialogues among bodies of Christians who, in former unhappy times, were bitterly at odds with one another is one positive sign. Another is the unprecedented theological consensus on Baptism, Eucharist, and Ministry in the Church which was reached in the World Council of Churches' consultations in Louisville, Kentucky (1979), and Lima, Peru (1982), among Orthodox, Protestant, Roman Catholic, and Anglican theologians. This achievement points up the potential to bring the fruit of various promising bilateral relationships into focus on a multilateral, pan-Christian basis. Whether or not it constitutes a lasting breakthrough remains to be seen.

Of similar potential influence towards theological and ecclesiastical convergence are the modern-day versions of the "Oxford Movement." These are diverse outcroppings in mainline Protestant denominations and parachurch groups known variously as "Orthodox Evangelicals" and "Renewalists":

> Hoping somehow to bump their church[es] off liberal tracks, and reroute [them] back toward historic roots ... the leaders [of these movements] are encouraged enough to stand their ground, anticipating that the flag of orthodoxy will yet be planted on surprising territory.[3]

Each of these movements is approaching the task of renewal in its own way and according to its diverse constituency's own lights. Staunch Reformation heirs that the majority of them are, many have begun, nevertheless, to mine the pastoral, conciliar, liturgical, homiletic, and ethical treasures of the ancient, pre-Reformation Church Fathers of East and West alike. In the process, they appear to be breathing new life into Christian witness today and particularly into the consciousness of their own denominational communions. In reaction against proliferating denominationalism, overzealous fundamentalism, and creedal and ethical liberalism, more and more Protestant conservatives "no longer relish their separation from other Christian believers."[4] Instead, they view true evangelical Christians as "agents of renewal within the one, holy, catholic and apostolic church."[5]

Orthodoxy and Contemporary Dialogues

Orthodoxy on her own part is engaged in several official dialogue partnerships aimed eventually at achieving organic church unity. In order of priority and likelihood of accomplishment, these include talks with: the ancient, pre-Chalcedonian Eastern Churches (the Armenian Apostolic Churches, the Coptic Churches of Egypt and Ethiopia, the Jacobite Churches of Syria and India, and the Assyrian Church of the East), the Polish National and other "Old Catholic" Churches of the West, the Roman Catholic Church, and the Anglican/Protestant Episcopal and Lutheran communions. With certain major families of the Protestant religious community that are associated traditionally with the "Radical Reformation"— most notably the Presbyterian, Calvinist Reformed, and (Ana)Baptist confessions—conversations are underway to bring about a basic measure of mutual understanding on key differences and perceptions of faith and practice.

On a worldwide basis and so far as a constant organic effort is concerned, the more promising of Orthodoxy's ecumenical endeavors and more readily approachable breaches are those with the ancient Eastern Churches and the Roman Catholic Church. With regard to the former, five universal dialogues took place in the 1960s and 1970s which "established that the differences between [the two sister families of Eastern Orthodox heritage] are not in faith, but in terminology . . . [and] it is our hope that this first major division between Christian churches may be healed soon, as an important step toward the full restoration of the visible unity of the church of Christ."[6] This is, again, in reference to the concept of reunion according to priority and affinity—by means of ever-widening, concentric circles of Christian unity, in recognition of existing commonality of heritage and proximity of ecclesial "family" in terms of shared faith and sacramental life. The Ecumenical Patriarchate and the worldwide pre-synodal committee of Orthodox Churches apparently share this concept. In their definitive 1976 planning sessions, they elected the ecumenical movement and certain bilateral dialogues as top priority on the agenda of the future pan-Orthodox ecumenical council.

Orthodox/Roman Catholic relations took on new hope and priority of effort with the election in 1978 of Polish Pope John Paul II, known to be deeply familiar with the Orthodox tradition and anxious to heal the medieval schism. The effort had languished in the uncertain years intervening since the Vatican II Council and the historic exchanges between Rome and Constantinople during the halycon decade of the 1960s. The energetic new Slavic pontiff and the Ecumenical Patriarchate, in consultation with leading Roman Catholic and Orthodox hierarchs and agencies, for the first time in 1,100 years established an equal ecumenical commission. This joint agency was mandated to develop a common agenda, to engage in dialogue on matters at issue, and to create processes that would resume the trek to a restored communion. On the initiative of Pope John Paul, two dramatic symbolic gestures have accompanied the resumption of talks and ecumenical relations. In November, 1979 he visited the embattled Ecumenical Patriarch Demetrios and the premier Church of Orthodoxy, on the Feast of Saint Andrew the Apostle, Patron of Byzantium. History was made especially by his synodal proclamation during the Pentecost 1981 Liturgy—in Greek and Latin alike—of the ancient Creed of the undivided Church in its original form, *without the addition of the divisive "Filioque" formula.*[7]

Certain fundamentally divergent attitudes and orientations have developed as a natural consequence of the churches' isolation during the centuries of schism. The principal items of contention, though, between the Orthodox and Roman Catholic Churches are: the "Filioque" question, the Roman papacy (disputed jurisdictional supremacy vs. accepted ecumenical primacy), the collegiality of the episcopacy, the anomaly of "Uniate" Eastern communities subject to Rome's rule, certain understandings of the sacraments and exercise of canonical *oikonomia,* and the nature of the Church and churches.[8] Despite such key matters at issue, some authorities still foresee this particular reunion being able to be achieved before the year 2,000 A.D.[9]

The dialogues with the "Old Catholic" churches date from the latter's original formation—in parts of Germany, Holland, Poland, Czechoslovakia, Switzerland, France, and America—as a consequence of their mid-nineteenth century break with the parent Church of Rome.[10] Sharing in the ancient Western Catholic tradition, these churches have developed an affinity towards Orthodoxy that has, especially in recent decades, quickened the dialogue. The relationships "continue [as] one of the most promising . . . between sister Churches . . . [in endeavoring to find] ways of healing old separations among them."[11] Their current partial ties with bodies of the Anglican/Protestant Episcopal and Lutheran communions also present a challenge to the Church's *oikonomia* in the event that an Orthodox/Old Catholic union were to take place.

Except for the Eastern Orthodox/Roman Catholic relationship, perhaps no ecumenical relationship in the Christian world has been more longlasting, high-level, and frequent in contact than the Orthodox encounters with the Anglican/Protestant Episcopal communion. But, equally so, none has proved to be more fraught with frustration and dashed hopes for the Orthodox, largely on account of the very history and constitutional nature of this hybrid family of like Christian episcopal communities.

Engendered in the midst of the Protestant Reformation, the independent Church of England nevertheless insisted—in opposition to the "Radical Reformers" of Scotland and continental Europe—on her right and need to retain much of the forms and confessional aspects of her ancient Western Catholic heritage, as the history of the controversial Book of Common Prayer has shown.

Under the influence of successive Protestant movements, hierarchs, and monarchs, certain modifications did take place in the old Catholic structure and ethos of the Church of England. This was evident especially in her ecclesial self-profession and sacramental understanding, the most significant alterations being the "Thirty-Nine Articles" which reflected most directly the Reformation side of her development. A counter-influence also came to bear through the agency of the Anglo-Catholic "Non-Juror" and "Oxford Tractarian" evangelical movements of the seventeenth and nineteenth centuries, respectively. England's daughter churches experienced a like history.

The Reformed Protestant and Anglo-Catholic orientations are the dissimilar twins which constitute poles of religious and ecclesiastical dichotomy in the ethos of the Anglican/Protestant Episcopal communion. The result has been a concept of "comprehensiveness," a wide and apparently contradictory variance in church life, and indefinable flexibility in interpretation and application of faith and order. The Orthodox and other churches of the Catholic tradition interpret this to mean that no patristic sense of the wholistic Covenant and, therefore, no *consensus fidelium* may ever ultimately prevail or be perceived as the definitive and authoritative canon of the communities' life. This continues as the practical as well as the philosophical stumbling-block in the way of unity. An all-inclusive Orthodox/Anglican "summit" dialogue, the fruit of the churches' four and a half centuries of ecumenical encounters took place in Moscow, Russia, in 1976. But the lack of an authoritative Anglican voice to affirm the mutually agreed findings, especially in view of the unilateral events and proclamations which took place in the American, Canadian, and other Anglican communities prior to and following the 1978 Lambeth Conference, have placed the very relationship in jeopardy.[12]

Following their sixteenth century revolt against Rome, the Reformers Martin Luther and Philipp Melanchthon early attempted to contact the Orthodox Church. The inability of the principals to confer in person and to speak some measure of common theological language, coupled with the ferocity of the Reformation at that period and the Ottoman Turk captivity of the ancient patriarchal sees, doomed the effort from inception. Centuries later, due largely to the resettlement after revolutions and two world wars of many Orthodox Christians in predominantly Protestant lands, encounter became inevitable. Initiatives in dialogue and common service programs have taken place between Lutherans and the Orthodox diaspora communities. The 1976 pre-synodal conference voted, therefore, to "make good use of the existing theological exchanges and to prepare for official [international] dialogue with the Lutheran Church."[13] The relative ecclesiastical stability, confessional self-perception, and integral sacramental understanding of the Lutheran communion, patricularly in northern Europe, have heightened the prospects for fruitful sharing and development of unity, and international dialogues are underway.

Finally, for the most part, the arena for dialogue with the main body of the heirs to the Protestant Reformation has been the Faith and Order Commission and other joint endeavors and assemblies of the World Council of Churches. Multilateral dialogues and, in that context, some resulting bilateral conversations have been the occasion for what exchange has generally taken place. Some conversations have also been held between Orthodox and Reformed (Presbyterian) theological institutes and seminaries. Similarly, in 1977 and 1981, pastors, college and seminary faculty, and staff of the Greek Orthodox Archdiocese and the Southern Baptist Convention in America engaged in common prayer and an exploratory dialogue. More such encounters are planned, in order to develop mutual understanding and gradually to broaden the degree of common exposure between Orthodox and their evangelical Christian brethren of Reformed tradition.

Orthodoxy's Ecumenical Task, and the American Opportunity

The language of the World Council of Churches' Fifth Assembly (Nairobi, 1975) paraphrased closely the ecumenical mandate as it was perceived by the Fathers of the Council of Carthage over fifteen centuries earlier: "[We] call the churches to the goal of visible unity in one Faith and in one eucharistic fellowship, expressed in worship and in common life in Christ, and to advance [by practical means] towards that unity in order that the world may believe."[14]

By consensus of ancient tradition, the major responsibility and prerogative for ecumenical initiatives and decision making belongs to the Ecumenical Patriarchate and the pan-Orthodox synod. It is likewise understood, however, as that same Council of Carthage affirmed, that the local churches bear a key responsibility: to meet ecumenical needs in their own areas and according to their particular resources and capability to contribute to the catholic effort of the whole Church. In response to the Nairobi call, the pan-Orthodox consultation on the ecumenical movement (New Valamo, Finland, 1977) further elaborated on this theme:

> The Church . . . of which the Eucharist is a manifestation (Cf. *Didache* 10) . . . is not an abstract or speculative idea, but a concrete reality . . . primarily identified with the local Eucharistic community in each place. . . .
>
> Even the divisions created by time and space have to be overcome in this community, . . . and although it is in fact a local community [as such], it offers the Eucharist in behalf of the entire *oikoumene,* thus acquiring truly ecumenical dimensions in which the divisions of space are also overcome. . . . Through the office of the bishop . . . in the episcopal diocese each Eucharistic gathering acquires its catholic nature . . . .
>
> This faithfulness to [the one Apostolic faith], however, must always be understood as a living continuity [of] two essential aspects: fidelity and renewal . . . in the spirit of creative obedience. Renewal thus comes to mean . . . responding to new, changing situations on the basis of the truth once given [and] the application of the Apostolic Tradition to contemporary questions and needs.[15]

This writer is convinced that, despite the diaspora communities' problems, it is the local churches in America that are uniquely suited to meet the contemporary needs of this special evangelical apostolate. More so than any other church in Orthodox Christendom, they are free from coercion, diverse, and ecumenical in exposure and relationships, potential and actual. They are situated in the heartland of a vigorous variety of expressions of Western Christianity—Protestant, Evangelical, and Catholic. It is, in short, an ideal setting for the practical application of the Church's ecumenical task and findings to date.

However, one of the major obstacles, especially in America, to Orthodoxy's participation in the ecumenical movement is that her Churches' resources are limited and dispersed. It follows, then, that—for the sake of their common mission and witness to Christ—America's Orthodox Churches are called to organize the ecumenical effort on a sustained basis: first, to set priorities, giving greater importance and allocation of resources to certain endeavors over others; second, to pool their existing resources to accomplish these priorities; and, third, to draw upon the dormant, largely untapped resources among the communities of the faithful, clergy and laity alike. In this way, Orthodoxy will be able to meet effectively both the opportunities at hand and those likely to arise in the future, as the very principles and canons of her ancient Covenant demand.

Consequently, in specific epilogue to this study and "in humility and a spirit of repentance,"[16] this writer respectfully recommends the following steps and programs for consideration in implementing Orthodoxy's ecumenical ministry in America:

I. Primary Ecumenical Relationships:

1. Creation of a four-partner, "Orthodox-Catholic Forum of Bishops," for purposes of shared pastoral consultation, common ecumenical witness, and closer fellowship between the canonical Eastern Orthodox Churches, the ancient Churches of the East, the Polish National and other "Old Catholic" Churches, and the Roman Catholic Church in America. The bishops would: consult at least once yearly on major contemporary pastoral and ethical issues confronting their faithful and offer, when possible, common pastoral guidance thereupon; to the extent possible, form a unified caucus of Orthodox-Catholic action and concern in the work of the National Council of Churches and other ecumenical organizations; and take the lead in ecumenical dialogue and pastoral life programs.

2. Give priority to pan-Orthodox dialogues and select common endeavors with the "Evangelical Orthodox" community, to give

support to them in their spiritual pilgrimage and pastoral needs and to clarify and resolve the issues which still remain in the way of reconciling them to canonical Orthodoxy.

3. Create ongoing forums for specialized bilateral dialogues with: (a) the Lutheran Council in the U.S.A.; (b) select Anglican/-Protestant Episcopal agencies; (c) the National Association of Evangelicals, and the Southern Baptist Convention; (d) the pan-Protestant "Consultation on Church Union"; and (e) representatives of the Orthodox, Conservative, and Reform traditions of Judaism.

4. Analyze and determine which activities and agencies of the National Council of Churches are most effective in terms of Orthodox participation and witness, so that our churches may give priority to them.

II. Developing "Grassroots" Ecumenism:

1. Develop three general-interest pamphlets, or guidebooks, for diocesan and parish community needs: (a) on the theme and basic roots of the Church's ecumenical tradition and history; (b) on the background, history, and current life of the basic Christian and Judaic denominations; and (c) on guidelines for "minimum expected" ecumenical relationships and activities.

2. Develop and conduct national, regional, and diocesan seminars on the above, for the training and guidance of clergy and lay leadership.

3. In order to strengthen the mutual understanding and encounter of the church communities represented in the "Orthodox-Catholic Forum of Bishops":

a. Select a portfolio of existing consensus, or agreed-statement, papers which reflect the common understandings and diverging positions of the participating churches on key theological, pastoral, and ethical issues.

b. Develop abridged texts and guidebooks on the above, for use by study groups.

c. From each participating church, select parishes or clusters of parish communities which, with the guidance of their respective bishops, will covenant to create area forums for study and prayer together throughout the Church Year on the questions raised in the ecumenical study guidebooks.

d. Explore the creation of inter-diocesan and parish-level joint "spiritual retreats," engaged-couples preparation, "marriage encounters," church school projects, campus ministries, clergy pastoral forums, and scheduled exchanges of visits between the participating churches.

A Postscript

The principal theme, indeed the hope, running through these proposals is the practical ecumenical benefit of common encounter and shared experiences which can result among the formerly disconnected churches of Orthodox and Catholic traditon. Veterans of the ecumenical movement readily witness that, if engaged in soberly and prayerfully on a regular basis, such encounter can bring about spiritual renewal, deeper understanding, and shared identification among the participants. After less than a decade of involvement in the embryonic ecumenical movement, in 1936 the late Professor Hamilcar Alivisatos expressed to his colleagues his surprise and enthusiasm over the results effected within Orthodox circles alone and in witness to other Christians:

> Whereas theologians from various parts of the Orthodox Church had previously been indifferent to one another, in these international conferences [they] banded together spontaneously and naturally to uphold Orthodox positions and constituted a united Orthodox group. . . .
>
> They thus attracted attention by presenting, within the bosom of the [wider] Christian family, a much clearer profile of an Orthodoxy which had been thought [by Protestants] to be moribund. . . . It is to the ecumenical movement that we owe the opportunity . . . which also holds such promise . . . for the future of the Christian family. . . .[17]

Speaking forty years later, Professor Vasilios Istavridis similarly credited the ecumenical movement, and the opportunities it provided for prayerful dialogue and shared experience, with having effected "the rebirth of Orthodox theology in the 20th century" and with having engendered a growing "inner unity" in spiritual life across the continent of Europe.[18]

This should not, however, be the experience or possession only of a fortunate elite; nor, conversely, should the reality of setbacks and confrontation with the difficulties of working out humankind's wider social and moral needs be theirs alone. The ecumenical "state of the art," with all its advantages and drawbacks, can and should be brought into the experience of the diocesan bishop, the parish presbyter, and the man, woman, and child "in the pews." The Great Commission, after all, was and is an evangelical imperative to all, "even these the least of my brethren." This is in order that the promise given to Noah, the Prophets, and all "who dwell in darkness" might be fulfilled in the one, holy, catholic, and apostolic Church which Jesus Christ has built upon the faith, hope, and love of all of His disciples.

*   *   *

TO THE GLORY

OF THE FATHER, OF THE SON, AND OF THE HOLY SPIRIT

THE ONE GOD.

Amen.

NOTES

[1]*In Search of Christianity: Discovering the Diverse Vitality of Christian Life,* by Ninian Smart (San Francisco, 1979), pp. 262-63, 305ff.

[2]"Christian Unity and Ecumenism," in *Documents of the Orthodox Church in America,* March 1973.

[3]"Pressing for Renewal in Mainline Churches," *Christianity Today,* May 7, 1982, p. 32.

[4]"The Split-Up Evangelicals," *Newsweek,* April 26, 1982, p. 91.

[5]Ibid.

[6]Bishop Maximos, ecumenical committee chairman of the Greek Orthodox Archdiocese Synod of Bishops, in "The Orthodox Church in Dialogue," *The Illuminator* (Diocese of Pittsburgh), February 1981, p. 12. See also: "Orthodox and Non-Chalcedonians Confer in Etchmiadzine, Armenia," *The Orthodox Church,* December 1975, p. 2.

[7]"Orthodox Hierarch Preaches at Saint Peter's; Pope John Paul Recites Creed Without 'Filioque,' " and "Signs of Hope In the Ecumenical Horizon," in *The Illuminator,* August-September 1981, pp. 1, 11.

[8]"Greek Orthodox Say Talks With Rome Falter," by Paul Anastasi, *The New York Times,* October 18, 1981. On the pioneer talks and promising agreed statements reached in the American dialogues, see "Orthodox-Roman Catholic Consultation," by Father Edward J. Kilmartin, S.J., *New Catholic World,* July-August 1977, pp. 179-80, 184-86.

[9]"Problems Remain in Ecumenical Talks": an interview with Archbishop Stylianos, co-chairman of the international Catholic-Orthodox Theological Commission, in the *National Catholic Register* of Australia, August 16, 1981; "Rome and Orthodoxy: Where Do We Go From Here?" editorial in *The Orthodox Church,* October 1981; "Orthodox and Catholics Take Steps Toward Unity," *Orthodox Observer,* October 21, 1981.

[10]"Towards the Great and Holy Council: Orthodoxy and the Other Churches," *Orthodox Observer,* September 28, 1977, pp. 2, 6.

[11]Bishop Maximos, "Orthodox Church," p. 12.

[12]Bishop Maximos, "Towards the Great and Holy Council . . . "

[13]Bishop Maximos, ibid.

[14]"Report of the Valamo Consultation: The Ecumenical Nature of the Orthodox Witness," in the *Greek Orthodox Theological Review*, 23 (1978) 174.

[15]Ibid., pp. 170-71.

[16]Bishop Maximos, "Living Orthodoxy: The Orthodox Church in Dialogue," *The Illuminator*, October 1980, p. 12.

[17]Quoted in "The Ecumenicity of Orthodoxy," *The Ecumenical Review*, 29 (1977) 182.

[18]Ibid., p. 192.

BIBLIOGRAPHY*

1. The Ecumenical Movement

Anderson, Gerald and Thomas F. Stransky, C.S.P. (eds). *Christ's Lordship and Religious Pluralism.* Baltimore, 1981.

Barrois, Dr. George. "Closed Communion, Open Communion, Intercommunion?" *St. Vladimir's Theological Quarterly,* 12 (1968) 142-56.

Blake, Dr. Eugene Carson. "The World Council of Churches: East-West Relations 1966-1972," *Voices of Unity: Essays in Honor of Willem Adolf Visser't Hooft* . . . Ans J. van der Bent (ed.). Geneva, 1981, pp. 1-10.

Calian, Dr. Carnegie Samuel. "Which Councils Are Ecumenical— From Nicaea to Vatican?" *The Greek Orthodox Theological Review,* 14 (1969) 181-97.

Congar, Yves, O.P. "Trials and Promises of Ecumenism," *Voices of Unity . . . ,* pp. 23-32.

Ecumenical Study Guide on the Eucharist. Garrison, N.Y., 1977.

Emilianos (Timiadis), Metropolitan of Calabria. "Neglected Factors Influencing Unity." *The Greek Orthodox Theological Review,* 14 (1969) 111-37.

Hopko, Thomas. "Upsala 1968." *St. Vladimir's Theological Quarterly,* 12 (1968) 125-41.

Horton, Dr. Walter M. *Christian Theology: An Ecumenical Approach.* New York, 1958.

*In addition to the sources cited in the body of this study (i.e., following each chapter).

Hotchkin, John F. "Christian Dialogue and the Eucharist," *Catholic Mind* (March 1977) 11-32.

Ignatios, Metropolitan of Lattakiah. "Behold, I Make All Things New," *St. Vladimir's Theological Quarterly,* 12 (1968) 108-19.

Lange, Ernest. *And Yet It Moves: Dream and Reality of the Ecumenical Movement.* Edwin Robertson, trans. Abridged by Dr. Konrad Raiser and Dr. Lukas Vischer. Belfast, 1979.

Meyendorff, John. "Unity of the Church—Unity of Mankind," *St. Vladimir's Theological Quarterly,* 15 (1971) 163-77.

Meyendorff. "Worship in a Secular World: An Introduction to the Work of the Assembly Section on Worship." *St. Vladimir's Theological Quarterly,* 12 (1968) 120-24.

Papaderos, Dr. Alexandros. "The Gadfly on Trial: the 'Political' Commitment of the World Council of Churches," *Voices of Unity* . . . pp. 78-91.

Rouse, Ruth and Stephen Neill (eds). *A History of the Ecumenical Movement, 1517-1948.* London, 1954.

Ware, Kallistos (Timothy). "Orthodoxy and the World Council of Churches." *Sobornost/Eastern Churches Review,* 1 (1979) 74-82.

Zernov, Dr. Nicholas. *Orthodox Encounter: The Christian East and the Ecumenical Movement.* London, 1961.

2. Church History and Patristics

Bromiley, Geoffrey W. *Historical Theology: An Introduction.* Grand Rapids, 1978.

Evans, Robert F. *One and Holy: The Church in Latin Patristic Thought.* London, 1972.

Florovsky, Georges. *Aspects of Church History.* Collected Works, Volume 4. Belmont, Mass., 1975.

Florovsky. *Bible, Church, Tradition.* Collected Works, Volume 1. Belmont, Mass., 1975.

Florovsky. *Christianity and Culture.* Collected Works, Volume 2. Belmont, Mass., 1975.

Galloway, A.D. (ed). *Basic Readings in Theology.* London, 1964.

Goguel, Maurice. *The Primitive Church.* London, 1964.

Green, Michael. *Evangelism in the Early Church.* Grand Rapids, 1970.

Merton, Thomas (M. Louis, O.C.S.O.), translator and commentator. *The Wisdom of the Desert: Sayings . . . of the Fourth Century.* London, 1974.

Pelikan, Dr. Jaroslav. *The Emergence of the Catholic Tradition (100-600).* Volume 1 of *The Christian Tradition.* Chicago, 1977.

Treadgold, Donald W. *A History of Christianity.* Belmont, Mass., 1979.

Waddell, Dr. Helen, translator and editor. *The Desert Fathers.* Ann Arbor, 1960.

3. Orthodoxy

Atiya, Aziz S. *A History of Eastern Christianity.* Notre Dame, 1968.

Brightman, F. E. *The Eastern Liturgies.* Volume 1 of *Liturgies Eastern and Western.* Oxford, 1896.

Handbook of American Orthodoxy. Cincinnati and Indianapolis: Forward Movement Publications, Protestant Episcopal Church in the U.S.A., 1972.

Iakovos (Canavaris), Metropolitan of Germany. " The Ecclesiology of Fr. Yves Congar: An Orthodox Evaluation," *The Greek Orthodox Theological Review,* 15 (1970) 85-106.

Ieronimos (Kotsonis), Archbishop of Athens and All Greece. *Problemata tes ekklesiastikes oikonomias.* Athens, 1957.

Istavridis, Vasilios T. "The Ecumenical Patriarchate," *The Greek Orthodox Theological Review,* 14 (1969) 198-225.

Maximos, Metropolitan of Sardes. *The Ecumenical Patriarchate in the Orthodox Church.* Analekta Vlatadon, 24. Thessalonike, 1976.

Meyendorff, John, (ed). "The Catholicity of the Church: A Symposium—Catholicity and the Structures of the Church, Catholicity and Ecumenism, and Catholicity and Mission," *St. Vladimir's Thelogical Quarterly,* 17 (1973).

Nissiotis, Dr. Nikos A. *Interpreting Orthodoxy . . . to Christians of Western Church Traditions.* Minneapolis, 1981.

Nissiotis, Dr. Nikos A. and Paul Verghese. "The Third and Fourth Consultations Between Eastern Orthodox and Oriental Orthodox Theologians, at Geneva and Addis Ababa," *The Greek Orthodox Theological Review,* 16 (1971).

Orthodoxy: A Faith and Order Dialogue (#30) Geneva, 1960.

"Papers Presented at the First International Theological Conference of Orthodox Theologians in America: 1970," *The Greek Orthodox Theological Review,* 17 (1972).

"Papers Presented at the Third International Theological Conference of Orthodox Theologians in America: 1978," *The Greek Orthodox Theological Review,* 24 (1979).

Paul, Archbishop of Finland. *The Faith We Hold.* Crestwood, N.Y., 1980.

Philippou, A.J. (ed). *Orthodoxy—Life and Freedom: Essays in Honor of Archbishop Iakovos.* Oxford, 1973.

Philippou. *The Orthodox Ethos: Essays in Honor of the Centenary of the Greek Orthodox Archdiocese of North and South America.* Oxford, 1964.

Schmemann, Alexander. *Church, World, Mission: Reflections on Orthodoxy in the West.* Crestwood, N.Y., 1979.

Schmemann, Alexander. *Liturgy and Life: Christian Development Through Liturgical Experience.* New York, 1974.

Stylianopoulos, Theodore, Demetrios J. Constantelos, and Dr. George Bebis. "The Authority of Tradition: A Symposium," *The Greek Orthodox Theological Review,* 15 (1970) 7-84.

Ware, Kallistos (Timothy). *The Orthodox Church.* Baltimore, 1969.

Ware. *The Orthodox Way.* London and Oxford, 1979.

Yearbook 1982. New York, Greek Orthodox Archdiocese of North and South America.

4. *Orthodoxy, Roman Catholicism, and Anglicanism*

Baker, Derek, (ed). *The Orthodox Churches and the West.* Volume 13 of *Studies in Church History.* Oxford, 1976.

Barrois, Dr. Georges. "Anglican-Orthodox Relations: Reflections of an Orthodox on Some Anglican Comments." *St. Vladimir's Theological Quarterly,* 15 (1971) 191-211.

"... *Be Reconciled to Your Brother*": *The Lifting of the Anathema of 1054 A.D. As a Step Toward Reconciliation.* New York, 1966.

Constantinople, The Great Church of (Ecumenical Patriarchate). *The Reply of the Orthodox Church to Roman Catholic Overtures on Reunion.* Orthodox Christian Movement of Saint John the Baptist. New York, 1958.

Guettee, Abbe Rene-Francois. *The Papacy: Its Historic Origin and Primitive Relations With the Eastern Churches.* New York, 1866.

Haugh, Dr. Richard. *Photius and the Carolingians: The Trinitarian Controversy.* Belmont, Mass., 1975.

Kilmartin, Edward J., S.J. *Toward Reunion: The Orthodox and Roman Catholic Relations.* New York, 1979.

Maguire, Kenneth (Anglican Bishop of Montreal). "Comments on Anglican-Orthodox Relations." *St. Vladimir's Theological Quarterly,* 15 (1971) 178-90.

Maximos IV (Sayegh), Melkite Catholic Patriarch of Antioch, (ed). *The Eastern Churches and Catholic Unity.* New York, 1963.

Methodios (Fouyas), Archbishop of Aksum. *Orthodoxy, Roman Catholicism and Anglicanism.* Brookline, 1985.

Ostroumoff, Ivan N. *The History of the Council of Florence.* Trans. Basil Popoff. Boston, 1971.

"The Monks of Mount Athos Speak on Roman Catholic-Orthodox Dialogue," *Bulletin of the Orthodox Theological Society of America* (January 1981) Lexington, Mass.

The Primacy of Peter in the Orthodox Church. Library of Orthodox Theology and Spirituality. London, 1973.

Vischer, Dr. Lukas, (ed). *Spirit of God, Spirit of Christ: Ecumenical Reflections on the Filioque Controversy.* Geneva, 1981.

Ware, Kallistos (Timothy) and Colin Davey (eds). *Anglican-Orthodox Dialogue: The Moscow "Agreed Statement."* London, 1977.

5. *Orthodoxy and Protestant Reformed Traditions*

Bachmann, Dr. Theodore. "Orthodoxy's Windows to the West: A New Center in Geneva," *Lutheran World,* 23 (1976) 186-87.

Berger, Peter L. and Richard J. Neuhaus (eds). *Against the World/For the World: The Hartford Appeal and the Future of American Religion.* New York, 1976.

Bobrinskoy, Boris. "The Trinitarian Approach in Orthodox Worship." *Lutheran World.* 23 (1976) pp. 171-74.

Bria, Ion. "Concerns and Challenges in Orthodox Ecclesiology Today." *Lutheran World.* 23 (1976) pp. 188-91.

Calian, Dr. Carnegie Samuel. *Icon and Pulpit: The Protestant-Orthodox Encounter.* Philadelphia, 1968.

Emilianos (Timiadis), Metropolitan of Calabria. "The Holy Spirit and the Mystical in Orthodox Theology," *Lutheran World.* 23 (1976) pp. 175-79.

Evdokimoff, Paul. "The Icon of the Holy Trinity," pp. 166-70.

Fueter, Paul. "Confessing Christ Through Liturgy: An Orthodox Challenge to Protestants," *Lutheran World,* 23 (1976), 180-85.

Gillquist, Dr. Peter. "The Evangelical Orthodox Church," *Theosis* (June 1980).

"Greek Orthodox/Southern Baptist Consultation," *The Greek Orthodox Theological Review,* 22 (1977).

Harakas, Stanley S. "Living the Orthodox Christian Faith in America." *Lutheran World,* 23 (1976), 192-99.

Martensen, Daniel F. "Introduction: Eastern Orthodoxy on Lutheran Agenda," *Lutheran World,* 23 (1976), 164-66.

"Martin Luther: His Views on the Orthodox Church," *Logos* (May 1969), pp. 13-15.

Meyendorff, John and Dr. Joseph C. McLelland (eds). *The New Man: An Orthodox and Reformed Dialogue.* New Brunswick, N.J., 1973.

Oden, Thomas C. *Agenda for Theology: Recovering Christian Roots.* San Francisco, 1979.

"Reports and Documentation: Lutheran/Russian Orthodox Conversations," *Lutheran World,* 23 (1976), 220-26.

Webber, Robert E. *Common Roots: A Call to Evangelical Maturity.* Grand Rapids, 1979.

Webber, Robert E. and Donald Bloesch (eds). *The Orthodox Evangelicals.* Nashville, 1978.

General Index

A

Agape, love, 84

akribeia, 81, 92, 108, **115-28; definition of, 115-7**

anamnesis (remembrance), 42, 74

Anglican/Protestant Episcopal churches 126, 156-7

"Apostolic Canons," 83-4, 93

Athanasios of Alexandria, Saint, 34, 35, 51, 102, 118, 120, 131, 133

Anastasios I of Rome, Saint, 107

Authority, Christ's, and of the Church, 47, 48, 49-50, 59, 63, 80-1, 131

B

Baptism, Eucharist, and Ministry ("BEM document"), 17, 21, 152

Barnabas, Saint, 56, 60

Basil of Caesarea (Cappadocia), Saint, 91, 102, 104, 112, 118, 120, 123-4, 130, 132

berit (συνθήκη), definition of, 26

Bible, not sole source of revelation, 137-38

Buber, Martin, 33

C

Carthage, council of, 98, 105-10, 111, 124, 158

Chalcedon, council of, 105, 125

"Christians before Christ," 87, 94

Christians in the world, 42-3, 50, 60, 66, 70-1, 85-7, 93, 103

Church, as Body of Christ, 61-2, 71, 73-6, 81, 82-3, 85, 88, 91, 136, 137, 138-9
lack of love; rigorist spirit in, 99-100, 101-2, 104
nature of, 137-39

Clement of Alexandria, Saint, 116, 130, 131

Clement of Rome, Saint, 85, 88, 93, 94

Commandment, the Great, of Christ, 76, 136

Commission, the Great, of Christ, 40, 49, 54, 57, 59, 164

Communion, intercommunion, 82, 92, 96, 137, 145-6, 152

koinonia, 144

consensus fidelium, 12, 16, 17, 91

consensus patrum, 79, 109

"Council of Renunion" 879-880 A.D., 111, 150

Covenant, 11, 12, 17, 26, 29, 31, 34-50, 54, 58, 59, 63, 67, 71, 81, 83, 110; archetype of, 39; as hallmark of Judaism and Christianity, 34; as universal mission,

Scriptural Index

17.26—84,94
33.11—84,94

Ezekiel
18.23—45

Daniel
3: "Song of the Three"—22,33
7.14—48,52

Hosea
6.6—47,52

Micah
6.6-8—37,47,52

Malachi
2.4-10, 15, 17—47,52

Wisdom
15.1-2—38

Ecclesiasticus (Sirach)
25.1—27

Zephaniah
3.9—22,33,65

Matthew
5.7,9—96,112
5.9—107
5.13—42
5.14-16—87,95
5.16—44
5.17,20—47,52
5.23-24—44
5.23-25—96.112

5.24—63
5.41—66
5.41-42—64
5.43-47—96,112
5.44-48—38
5.48—96.112
6.25-34—69
7.12—44
7.26-27—44
7.28-29—48,52
9.9-13—35,51
9.13—120
9.35-37—36
10.8, 14-15, 40-49
10.24—47
12.25-26—42
12.48-50—38
13.52—18
15.1-20—47,52
15.32—36
16.13-14—43
16.13, 16-18—43,81,92
18.6-14—61
18.7—89
18.18-22—50,56,81,92
18.20—146
21.18-22—40,51
22.36-40—47,52
23—47,52
25.14-30—69
26.26-29—74,78
26.55—87,95
26.36-65—48,52
28.18—50
28.18-19—81,92
28.19—50,59,77

Parallel Texts Cited

Old Testament
Creation of Humankind
Gen 1.26-28/5.1-2—22,33

Judgement and Justice
Gen 18.21,25; Ezek 18.23 (cf.
Mt 7.12, Lk 6.37-8) — 44-5

Shema of Israel, Ist Commandment
Lev 18.5, 19.8; 1 Sam 15.22;
Is 29.13; Hos 6.6; Mic 6.6-8;
Mal 2.4-10, 15, 17 (cf. Mt 5.17-
20, 22.36-40/Mk 12.28-34/Lk 10.
25-28)—46-7,51

"Song of the Three"
Ps 96.1/Dan 3—22,33

Salvation for those "who dwell
in darkness" Is. 9.1-2 (cf. Lk
1.79)—39

Creation, Mission of Humankind
Is 42.6-7/61.1—22,33

Prophecy of Lord's Adoption of
Gentiles Is 44.5, 56.7-8; Zeph
3.9—65